PROGRESS IN PLANNING
Volume 1, Part 2

Editors:
D. R. DIAMOND and J. B. McLOUGHLIN

OFFICE
LINKAGES AND LOCATION

PC - II - 153

Hinweiskarte: En - D - II - 3

Contents of Volume 1

OFFICE LINKAGES AND LOCATION

A Study of Communications and Spatial Patterns in Central London

by

J. B. GODDARD

London School of Economics and Political Science

PERGAMON PRESS

Oxford · New York
Toronto · Sydney · Braunschweig

Pergamon Press Ltd., Headington Hill Hall, Oxford

Pergamon Press Inc., Maxwell House, Fairview Park, Elmsford,
New York 10523

Pergamon of Canada Ltd., 207 Queen's Quay West, Toronto 1

Pergamon Press (Aust.) Pty. Ltd., 19a Boundary Street,
Rushcutters Bay, N.S.W. 2011, Australia

Vieweg & Sohn GmbH, Burgplatz 1, Braunschweig

First edition 1973

Library of Congress Catalog Card No. 73—66

Printed in Great Britain by Page Bros (Norwich) Ltd

ISBN 0 08 017180 X

Office Linkages and Location

*A Study of Communications and
Spatial Patterns in Central London*

J. B. GODDARD

London School of Economics and Political Science

Contents

Preface

IN SPITE of a well-developed theory concerning activity location within city centres, reaching back to Robert Murray Haig's classic essay on *Understanding the Metropolis,* very few attempts have been made to study comprehensively the structure of a world metropolitan centre. Probably the most outstanding contributions have been the monographs that formed part of the New York Metropolitan Regional Study completed during the 1950s (Haig's essay, incidentally, formed part of an earlier New York regional study) and John Rannell's study of the urban core of Philadelphia. A metropolitan city centre demonstrates within a relatively small area all the basic dimensions of urban structure — of aggregate land-use patterns expressed in terms of a slowly changing stock of accommodation through which a more rapidly changing body of activities passes; of activity clusters expressed in terms of linkages through the movement of goods, people and information; and the competition for space, invasion and succession. But the very concentration and variety of activities involved in these dynamic processes makes the metropolitan centre a very difficult area to study empirically.

As a naïve research student undaunted by problems of concept, data and methods of analyses, I embarked in 1965 on a study of the activity structure of Central London. The first step was to reduce conceptually the complexity of the problem by viewing the structure of the city centre as composed of four interrelated but separately identifiable sub-systems: a stock of physical structures; the activities that occupy this stock; the spatial network of functional interdependencies linking these activities; and the spatial pattern of movements produced by interdependencies between activities with discrete geographical locations.

My first step was an analysis of aggregate land-use patterns within the centre, relating a broad classification of activities to the physical stock of accommodation. This identified office space as a key structural element in Central London; subsequent analysis therefore concentrated on office activity. The next step was a study of the processes by which activities pass through a relatively fixed stock of accommodation as expressed by the birth, migration and death of new offices. This study of changing office location identified the importance of the business 'cluster' containing groups of seemingly related offices. In order to examine such clusters more rigorously, especially the pattern of spatial association between different offices, a detailed study was made of location patterns within one part of Central London, basically the financial district of the City of London. This pilot study developed methods for identifying the activities that were members of different spatial clusters.

Distinctive patterns of localisation are a response to functional linkages between different types of offices, and these in turn lead to correspondingly structured patterns of

A*

movement within the centre. An analysis of taxi-flows within Central London revealed a number of movement systems which corresponded well to the structural regions identified in the earlier analysis of land-use patterns.

At this point, two links were missing from the original framework. These were a complete set of office employment data to extend the pilot study of spatial linkages from the City of London to the entire Central Area. And, secondly, some indication of the pattern of functional interdependencies, measured in terms of information flows, between different office activities.

The study presented in this monograph is concerned with providing these two links. It was supported by the South-east Economic Planning Council and carried out in the Geography Department at the London School of Economics during the period 1969-71. The subject was seen to be of significance to the Council because of the strategic importance of Central London to the whole South-east region. With an established policy of office dispersal from London, some guidelines as to which office activities most needed a central location were urgently required. Obviously the strength of communication ties not only to the centre at large, but perhaps to a particular part of it, were thought of as possible indicators of opportunities for dispersal. And in terms of operating a dispersal policy within the framework of a planned economic structure for Central London vis-à-vis the rest of London and the South-east, some information on the distribution of office employment between different activities and locations within the centre was obviously important. This monograph is a summary of a three-volume report covering the spatial analysis of office location within Central London, the communications survey and statistical appendices. Further details of the result and methods employed are given in these volumes. A limited number of copies are available from the Secretary to the South-east Economic Planning Board at the Department of the Environment.

A large number of people have contributed to this research study both directly and indirectly. I would first like to thank the staff of the South-east Regional Office at the Department of the Environment, particularly Clifford Curry and John Glester for their comments during all stages of the project. I also wish to thank the officers of the Central London boroughs for permission to have access to the office employment data and for their assistance in its collection.

Numerous research assistants worked on this project at various stages. In particular I would like to thank Laurie Baker and Richard Hilton who were responsible for much of the data analysis, and Elizabeth Essex and Diana Morris who carried out the survey of communications. The completion of the project would not have been possible without the help of Janet Fox and her secretarial colleagues in the Geography Department and Eunice Wilson and the staff of the Drawing Office. Finally, a number of people have made significant contributions to the design and analysis of the communications survey. In particular, I am indebted to Bertil Thorngren of the Stockholm School of Economics who has pioneered the field of communications studies in relation to location. He has been a continuing source of inspiration and guidance. Nearer to home, Alex Reid, Martin Elton, Hugh Collins and Roger Pye of the Communications Studies Group at University College, London, have helped in numerous ways, not least through their significant contributions to the study of impact of telecommunications on business contact patterns.

J.B. GODDARD.

London School of Economics and
        Political Science.

Introduction

THIS study was prompted by a number of basic questions concerning office location in Central London and the office employment structure of the Central Area in particular. In spite of the growing importance of office employment nationally and the realisation that the creation of office jobs can make a significant contribution towards regional employment problems, very little is known about the nature of the ties that confine nearly one out of every seven office workers in England and Wales to the 10 square miles of Central London (Rhodes and Kan, 1971; Cowen *et al.,* 1969). Such figures immediately raise the question of how essential is it for all of this office employment to be so concentrated, and makes the assessment of locational priorities for Central London a matter of national importance. Although strict central government controls on office development have been in operation in London and the South-east region for 8 years, few objective criteria have been formulated to assess the appropriateness of one type of office activity rather than another for a Central London location. Similarly, within Greater London, the Greater London Development Plan has declared as a key objective that 'the activities that need to be in Central London should be given opportunities to develop' (GLC, 1970). But while supporting the need for a selective approach towards planning the economic structure of Central London, there is at present little evidence as to what activities should be encouraged or discouraged and by what criteria appropriateness for the centre is to be assessed (Goddard, 1970a).

Obviously the importance of a particular activity can only be judged in a context of the overall economic structure of Central London, about which very little data is available. So before the more general question concerning locational ties can be considered, the information gap concerning the variety of office functions at present located in Central London needs to be filled. While very little in detail is known about the overall employment structure of Central London, even less information is available about the distribution of this employment within the Central Area. Such data may, at first sight, only seem to be relevant for local structure planning. But it can be argued that local decisions that could affect the employment structure of such a vital area are also of city-wide, regional and even national significance. This is partly because certain office activities might not only be tied to the Central Area at large but to particular locations within it; so patterns of internal location could be related to the more general issue of locational ties.

In part this paucity of basic data can be attributed to the problem of identifying office employment within the framework of product-based standard employment classifications. For instance, nearly one-quarter of Central London's office employment in 1966 was classified under three subdivisions of Minimum List Headings in the Standard Industrial Classification. While 'office employment' mainly refers to the type of job an individual does, and as such can be identified from a classification of occupations, it is still important to know the function of the business within which the occupation is pursued. Because office employment has been presented as a poorly differentiated form of activity in such sources as the Census, it has previously not been possible to pay much attention to the functional differences between offices. But in the city centre particularly these functional differences can be of major significance because the activities of one type of office establishment are frequently complementary to those of another. This complementarity — which frequently enables firms to derive certain external economies — gives rise to recurrent interaction between different offices, in the form of information flows, especially through personal contacts (Thorngren, 1967).

It is thus a well-established fact that one of the principal advantages of a central location is the ease with which personal contact can be maintained with customers and suppliers, especially where highly specialised services are involved. For instance, a recent survey sponsored by the Location of Offices Bureau of those firms which approached the Bureau for advice about decentralisation and then decided not to move, showed that personal contact with other businesses was the main reason for not moving. In addition to customers, offices are often involved in contacts not directly related to the sale and purchase of goods or services. In particular, through perhaps somewhat random contact with the economic and social environment made possible by the concentration of a wide range of functions in the metropolitan centre, an organisation may be able to adjust to changes in these environments and so ensure its long survival (Thorngren, 1970).

The central areas of large cities therefore consist of complex communication networks. Within such networks, aggregate information flows are unlikely to be random. Given the specific nature of complementarities, one would expect that certain groups of office functions are closely linked to one another and have far weaker connections with functions that fall into other groups. Thus the 'products' of one office establishment may be the 'inputs' of another. (In addition, some functions may have no significant pattern of information linkages). The network of linkages between functions may therefore be defined as a system within which there are a number of interrelated subsystems. Such subsystems can be regarded as office complexes, analogous in many respects to industrial complexes (Isard, 1960; Baker and Goddard, 1972). One of the basic objectives of this study has been to identify such complexes through the measurements of the linkages between different types of offices and to specify the strength of these links, particularly how far they depend on close spatial proximity.

Two complementary approaches to this problem have been adopted, and these form the basis of the two sections of this study. First, following Rannel's argument that location within the centre might in part reflect the linkage patterns of offices, a detailed analysis of the location of different categories of office employment in Central London has been undertaken (Rannels, 1956). This involved developing a more detailed classification of offices in order to facilitate a disaggregation of the heterogeneous employment classification categories of the Standard Industrial Classification. From the registrations of office establishments under the terms of the Offices, Shops and Railway Premises Act 1963, it has been possible to assign all such establishments to this new 196 category classification and also to pinpoint their location within the Central Area. These data form the basis of a more detailed description of the overall office employment structure of Central London. With information on approximately 32,000 separate establishments allocated to a fine geographical subdivision of the area, the location of different types of employment within the centre is then examined. More specifically, the degree of internal localisation of each type of employment has been precisely described and particular areas of concentration and specialisation identified. It has also been possible to see how far employment of each type co-varies spatially with employment of other types and so isolate office activities with similar patterns of locational association.

In such a spatial analysis, functional associations can only be inferred. Spatial relations do not necessarily imply that the office types concerned have any linkage ties in terms of information flows. So the second, and more important, part of the study is concerned with an attempt to measure the pattern of personal contact through meetings and telephone calls between offices in Central London. The Offices, Shops and Railway Premises Act register of establishments has been used to select a stratified sample of offices within which a further selection of executives recorded details of their business contacts in a specially designed contact diary. The final sample consisted of some 700 executives from 72 offices who, over a 3-day period, recorded details of 5500 telephone calls and 1800 meetings with persons outside their firms.

This survey established basic facts like Who contacts who, and where? That is, the volume of contacts between different office sectors and different areas within and outside London. This information is used to determine the extent to which different office sectors are involved in an identifiable contact network and particularly how far the pattern of locational groupings corresponds to sets of functionally linked offices. This analysis suggests a number of possible indicators on which a selective policy of office dispersal could be based. On the basis of such indicators it can be argued that loss of employment through decentralisation of an activity belonging to a particular office complex might seriously undermine the viability of the complex as a whole since each activity offers important external economies to other members of the group. In contrast, the loss of employment in weakly connected sectors is likely to have less far-reaching repercussions on the rest of the system. However, an increase in central employment in such sectors could have undesired side effects on the strongly linked activities by adding unnecessarily to their share of the congestion costs of the centre in terms of higher prices for land, labour and other factors.

However, before developing a locational policy based on linkage, account also has to be taken of the strength of these linkages in terms of how far they demand close spatial proximity. One of the chief criticisms of a linkage approach is that existing patterns of contact might in no way reflect an optimal location with respect to currently available, — let alone future — telecommunications technology. In the final part of the study the characteristics of communication links are examined to ascertain whether in fact they exhibit features of sub-optimality — i.e. to establish whether existing links can be stretched over space, particularly through use of telecommunications, without imposing serious diseconomies on the activities concerned. By adding features contact, like length, number of people involved and subject-matter discussed, to the analysis of inter-office communication, an attempt has been made to devise some weighting of these linkages in terms of the need for contacts to take the form of face-to-face meetings.

This weighting is suggested by way of a classification of contacts which relates not only to the mode of communication but also to the fundamental organisational processes to which these contacts are connected. Although new technological developments like videophones are likely to have an impact on business communications, the implication of such developments on office location in the city centre are not likely to be fully understood unless existing contact patterns are seen within a broader organisational framework.

PART I

Office Employment in Central London: A Spatial Analysis

CHAPTER 1

The Office Employment Structure of Central London

THE DATA PROBLEM

The object of this chapter is to provide a statistical framework within which the subsequent analysis of location and contact patterns can be set. Prior to this study very little was known in detail about the distribution of employment in Central London between different office activities. While the Minimum List Headings of the Census do give some indications, in the financial and service sectors the classification is far too broad; in the manufacturing sectors it is impossible to separate factory operatives from office workers. This latter difficulty was partly overcome by special tabulations of the 1966 Census giving occupational data by place of work, and from these data it was possible to identify office occupations for broad groupings of business sectors. While office employment basically refers to the job function of the employee, it is also important to know the type of business within which this individual is working. For example, while there are considerable similarities in the job functions of all computer managers, it is also significant whether the individual concerned is working in a computer bureau or a bank. Ideally, one would like data referring both to occupation and type of business. Failing this, a very detailed classification of the nature of business is probably the best indicator of the overall functions of an office establishment. As a final requirement, in view of the fact that location within a large metropolitan centre could be an important guide to linkage patterns, it is essential to establish to some degree of detail the location of different types of offices within the centre.

THE OFFICES, SHOPS AND RAILWAY PREMISES DATA

Many of these requirements were met in this study by the registration of office establishments under the terms of the Offices, Shops and Railways Premises Act. This Act is akin to the Factory Acts in that it lays down minimum standards for such premises. Forms are returned to local health authorities indicating, amongst other things, total office employment and nature of business. In theory, this should amount to a continuous registration of establishments, but in practice, because of problems of enforcement with the large number of establishments in Central London, there are always delays in updating the register. That is, delays in deleting forms for firms that have moved out of old premises or firms moving into new premises, or delays in notification of increases in employment. Even though there are small problems of reliability, these registers do provide a unique source of information concerning the functional and spatial structure of office employment in Central London.

In order to make maximum use of this detail, a four-digit classification of office employment was devised involving 196 categories. (Appendix A). These in turn could be aggregated into 87 three-digit and 22 two-digit categories. This classification was based upon the Minimum List Headings of the Standard Industrial Classification, taking due regard to the particular employment structure of Central London as indicated by the 1966 Census. Thus a policy of amalgamation of Minimum List Headings was adopted in the industrial sectors which are generally less well represented in Central London than nationally, while within the financial and service sectors Minimum List Headings were extensively subdivided. Details of 32,000 commercial office establishments were thus classified during 1968 and data aggregated for two separate systems of areal units — 112 500-m grid squares and 69 traffic zones. In addition, data were also collected from the Factory Inspectorate of employment in offices attached to factories and in central and local government offices.

OFFICE EMPLOYMENT AS INDICATED BY THE CENSUS

From special tabulations of the occupation tables of the 1966 Census it is possible to obtain a very broad picture of the localisation of office employment in Central London and its office employment structure. The concentration of office employment in the South-east region of England, Greater London and Central London can be seen in Table 1.

TABLE 1. *The Localisation of Office Occupations in Central London, 1966.*

Area	All office workers (000's)	Percentage of England and Wales		Office workers as per cent of total
		All employment	Office workers	
Central London	757	6	15	57
Greater London	1532	19	30	35
South-east region	1882	35	47	24
England and Wales	5089	100	100	19[a]

Source: 1966 Census and Strategic plan for the South-east. *Studies*, Vol. 1, HMSO.

[a] Fifteen per cent excluding South-east.

The table shows that the South-east region has 35% of all employment in England and Wales but 47% of all office employment. This concentration increases within London as a whole until in Central London one finds 15% of the country's office workers. The corollary of this concentration is that the occupational structure of each area in turn is increasingly dominated by office jobs (Table 2). Nonetheless, Central London is by no means devoted exclusively to office activity. Of the 1⅓ million people working in this area in 1966, 56% were in office occupations. Three-quarters of these were in clerical jobs and one-quarter in administrative and professional grades. Of the remainder of the workers in Central London, significant proportions can still be classified as factory operatives in addition to the large number of sales workers.

The distribution of these office workers between broad sector groups is given in Table 3. Not surprisingly, office workers are most important in finance, professional and

TABLE 2. *The Occupational Structure of Central London, 1966*

Occupational group	Central London		Greater London (%)	South-east region (%)	England and Wales (%)
	000's	%			
Operatives	220	17	32	36	44
Office workers:	757	57	35	29	22
(a) Administrative and professional	239	18	12	9	8
(b) Clerical	518	39	23	19	15
Transport	64	5	6	5	5
Sales	122	19	12	12	12
Others	177	13	16	18	16

Source: 1966 Census and Strategic plan for the South-east. *Studies,* Vol. 1, HMSO.

TABLE 3. *Office Occupations by Sector,*
Central London and Greater London, 1966

Sector	Office workers (000's)	Office workers as percentage of all workers	
		Central London	Greater London
Primary	5	61	35
Manufacturing	121	47	28
Construction	20	40	30
Services	610	60	38
Services, of which:			
Utilities, transport	89	54	38
Distribution	71	38	23
Finance, professional and scientific	260	79	52
Miscellaneous	102	47	30
Public administration	88	74	55

Source: 1966 Census and Strategic plan for the South-east. *Studies,* Vol. 1, HMSO.

scientific services and public administration. In all sectors, office jobs account for a far larger share of all employment in Central London than in Greater London as a whole. Thus 47% of workers in manufacturing industries in Central London are in office occupations compared with 28% in Greater London as a whole.

This pattern of concentration is far from static. The 5-year period preceding 1966 saw some redistribution of office employment away from Central London to other areas in Greater London, but particularly to the rest of the South-east region. Overall, employment in Central London has increased by some 65,000 (Table 4).

TABLE 4. *Changes in the Localisation of Office Occupations by Grade, 1961–1966*

Grade	Central London		Rest of Greater London	
	000's	%	000's	%
Administrative and professional	+19	9	+60	28
Clerical	−16	−3	+65	15
All office workers	+3	−	+125	19
All occupations	−65	−5	+131	4

Source: 1966 Census and Strategic plan for the South-east. *Studies*, Vol. 1, HMSO.

TABLE 5. *Changes in the Localisation of Office Occupations by Sector, 1961–1966*

Sector	Office workers 000's	Non-office workers 000's	Total 000's
Primary and manufacturing	−21	−35	−56
Construction	−1	−4	−5
Services, of which:	+15	−20	−5
Utilities, transport	−1	−11	−12
Distribution	−11	−13	−24
Finance and professional	+16	+11	+27
Miscellaneous	+6	−8	−2
Public administration	+3	+2	+5

Source: 1966 Census and Strategic plan for the South-east. *Studies*, Vol. 1, HMSO.

Office employment has shown a marginal increase representing the balancing out of two contrasting forces, namely a considerable increase of employment in administrative and professional grades and a decrease in clerical grades. The rest of London increased its office employment in both categories, but especially in the clerical grade. In the rest of the South-east region outside London it was again the growth of clerical office employment that was principally responsible for an overall increase in the number of office jobs.

In Table 5 these changes in office employment are broken down according to sector groups. The table shows that office employment in manufacturing (principally the administrative offices of firms with plants outside Central London) and wholesale and retail distribution had increased considerably, while in the financial and professional services there has been a marked increase of both office and non-office workers.

A final picture emerges of a very high concentration of office jobs in Central London, especially in financial and professional services, but a slight decline in the concentration of clerical employment, especially in the administrative offices of manufacturing firms. In part these changes can be attributed to the actual decentralisation of office establishments. According to the records of the Location of Offices Bureau, which takes the picture beyond 1966, 84,254 office jobs were decentralised by firms taking advice from the Bureau during the period from 1963 to 1972. (This represents an unknown proportion of the total amount of decentralisation). The bulk of these moves were partial decentralisations, particularly of routine and clerical jobs, and 47% of them were short-distance moves to other areas in Greater London (Rhodes and Kan, 1971). Of the jobs decentralised, 43% were in manufacturing and construction, 18% insurance, and 10% in distribution, indicating that in the financial sector there is also a considerable scope for decentralisation.

OFFICE EMPLOYMENT AS INDICATED BY THE OFFICES, SHOPS AND RAILWAY PREMISES ACT DATA

Using Census data it is only possible to obtain a very crude break-down of office employment. More detailed figures are available from the OSRP data, but there are questions of reliability. It is difficult to check reliability against the Census owing to differences in the classification of office employment, one being a work-place and the other an occupational definition. There are also differences in dates. Nevertheless, Table 6

TABLE 6. *A Comparison of Offices, Shops and Railways Premises Act and Census, Office Employment Figures*

Sector	1966 Census (000's)	OSRP (000's)	Difference (OSRP − Census)
Primary	5	3	−2
Manufacturing	121	115	−6
Construction	20	18	−2
Public utilities, transport	89	66	−23
Distribution	71	83	+12
Finance and professional	260	254	−6
Miscellaneous service	102	121	+19
Public administration	88	156	+68

Source: 1966 Census and Strategic plan for the South-east. *Studies,* Vol. 1, HMSO, and OSRP data (detached commercial offices, factory attached offices and central and local government offices).

B

indicates that the OSRP data represents an overestimate of office employment when compared with the 10% sample Census of 1966. When divided into broad sector groupings, the correspondence between Census and OSRP data is fairly close, especially in the critical financial and professional service sectors. In manufacturing, the correspondence is good if detached offices, which are the focus of this study, are considered in isolation. Taking the total employment in individual Census Minimum List Headings for the pure office sector and making comparisons for the equivalent OSRP categories also indicates a reasonable degree of accuracy in the OSRP data (Table 7).

A final test can be made concerning the distribution of employment within Central London by comparing the OSRP data with data on office floor-space, produced by the GLC for its 1966 land-use survey. Total office employment for each of the 112 grid squares was compared in a correlation analysis to reveal a high degree of association ($r = 0.95$). This is most encouraging for the subsequent spatial analysis since, unlike the previous comparisons, account is taken of geographical variations in reliability. Generally, these variations can be attributed to differences in the intensity of occupation of office space in various parts of Central London.

TABLE 7. *A Comparison of Office Employment Totals for Selected 1966 Census Minimum List Headings and the Corresponding Office, Shops and Railway Premises Act Categories*

Sector	1966 Census (000's)	OSRP (000's)	Difference (OSRP – Census)	Difference (%)
Insurance	76·9	70·3	−6·6	−8·6
Banking	64·6	67·4	+3·2	+4·8
Finance	24·2	25·9	+1·7	+7·2
Property	12·1	14·2	+2·1	+17·4
Accounting	23·8	20·6	−3·2	−13·4
Legal services	23·5	18·7	−4·8	−20·2
Scientific and technical services	25·7	26·1	+0·4	+1·6
Research and development	2·6	3·4	+0·7	+28·1
Professional and scientific organisations	3·8	3·8	−0·0	−0·7
Trade associations and business services	65·0	69·8	+4·8	+7·3

Source: 1966 Census (Industry tables) and OSRP.

THE STUDY AREA

The study area is described in Fig. 1, and variations in office employment density are described in Fig. 2. In collecting the OSRP data, the Registrar-General's definition of the Central Area made for purposes of the 1961 Census and widely adopted in planning studies since then, was taken as the study area. The data were grouped for 500-m grid squares, of which 112 out of 120 possible cells completely or partly in the Central Area, contained office employment. Within this area there are considerable variations in the density of office employment (including government offices and offices attached to factories), from over 20,000 persons per grid cell (320,000 per square km) in the City of London to less than 1000 (6000 per square km) in cells bordering the Central Area. Figure 2 shows secondary peaks of employment concentration in the Aldwych-Kingsway area and in Victoria which correspond to particular concentrations of office floor space (Goddard, 1967). North of Oxford Street – High Holborn, and South of Victoria Street and the river, office employment falls off sharply.

THE SIZE DISTRIBUTION OF OFFICE ESTABLISHMENTS

The OSRP data allows a break-down of total employment according to the size of the office establishment. This does not, of course, represent the full employment of the establishment as non-office workers like sales and canteen staff are excluded. Table 8 shows office employment and number of establishment by separate size groups. The most striking feature of the distribution is that 69% of the Central London establishments employ less than 10 office workers. In other words two-thirds of these establishments (24,000 out of 35,000) account for less than one-tenth of total office employment (73,000 out of 839,000). The converse is that 547 establishments each employing over 250 people account for over 40% of the total office employment. Table 8 shows that there are some differences between the various categories of offices, with factory-attached offices showing an even higher proportion of small establishments. In contrast, central and local government is dominated by very large establishments.

There are some variations in the distribution of small, medium and large establishments within the centre. Areas like the West End and Bloomsbury are characterised by relatively large shares of employment in small establishments, while the City, Victoria and Westminster have a large share of employment in establishments of over 250 persons.

It should be stated at this point that the data do not refer to firms. An establishment is a physically and functionally separate unit. Thus one firm may have its offices in adjacent, but separate office blocks, and these would be recorded as two units; conversely, another office building may contain a mixture of completely independent firms together with parts of firms with other offices elsewhere in London. Because there are no data on the distribution of firms sizes, we cannot say for certain what proportion of the large number of very small units represent independent firms. It is probably safe to assume that some proportion of this figure can be attributed to larger firms being forced to scatter their departments amongst a number of buildings. (The data therefore would support the findings of a recent Location of Offices Bureau survey, which suggested that one of the most important reasons for decentralisation is the need to bring scattered departments under one roof).

The remainder of the small units must represent a large number of small firms, and this does lend support to the notion that one of Central London's key roles is as a 'seed-bed' for

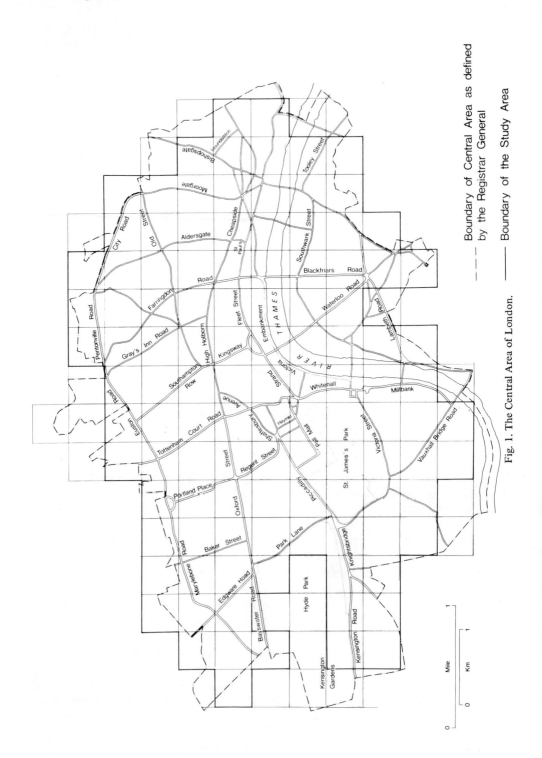

Fig. 1. The Central Area of London.

- - - -   Boundary of Central Area as defined
          by the Registrar General
———   Boundary of the Study Area

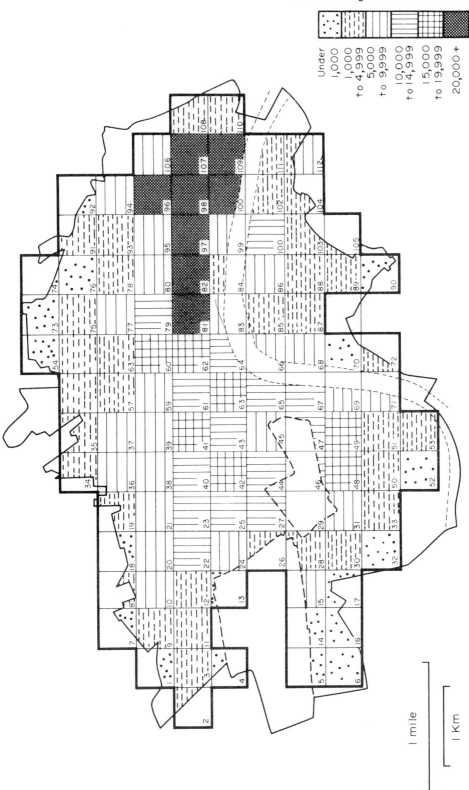

Fig. 2. Total office employment.

TABLE 8. *Office Employment and Number of Establishments*
by Size Group of Establishment

	Employment		Establishments	
	000's	%	No.	%
Detached commercial offices size group				
1–10	66·5	10·1	22,013	69·3
11–25	82·3	12·6	4,991	15·7
26–50	82·3	12·6	2,286	7·2
51–100	92·0	14·0	1,299	4·1
101–150	51·2	7·8	415	1·3
151–250	74·5	11·4	388	1·2
250+	207·0	31·6	383	1·2
Total	656·0	100·0	31,775	100·0
Factory attached offices				
1–10	5·9	22·0	1,792	81·3
11–25	4·3	15·9	266	12·1
26–50	2·9	10·9	81	3·7
51–100	2·3	8·4	32	1·4
101–150	1·5	5·6	12	0·5
151–250	1·2	4·6	6	0·3
250+	8·7	32·6	15	0·7
Total	27·0	100·0	2,204	100·0
Central and local Government offices				
1–10	0·9	0·6	188	24·2
11–25	1·8	1·1	103	13·3
26–50	4·1	2·6	112	14·4
51–100	7·9	5·1	111	14·3
101–100	7·7	4·9	62	8·0
151–250	10·3	6·6	51	6·6
250+	124·0	79·1	149	19·2
Total	157·0	100·0	776	100·0

Source: OSRP data.

new office activity. Although large firms may be short of the appropriate-sized accommodation, there is a clear case for the provision of office space in small units; and it is usually this form of accommodation that is lost in redevelopment schemes. Large-scale redevelopments for single firms have a further disadvantage in the form of limited local multiplier effects: large office complexes occupied by a single firm are usually self-contained in most respects. In addition to providing restaurant facilities, other personal services are often provided by the firm, e.g. barbers and hairdressers. On the commercial side, there is a greater chance that a large firm will provide its own business services rather than obtaining these from outside agencies. Large firms therefore reduce the richness of linkages within the city centre.

The distribution of office employment and establishments between different sectors can now be described in more detail than was possible using Census data. Table 9 gives a breakdown of employment in detached commercial offices for 22 two-digit groups of the OSRP classifications. The data confirm the importance of insurance, banking and finance and professional services in the office employment structure of Central London: these categories together accounting for one-third of all office jobs. Other important sectors are transport and communication, business services, entertainment, publishing, chemicals, societies and associations and commodity dealing.

TABLE 9. *Total Office Employment and Number of Establishments by Two-digit Sectors*

Sector	Total employment (000's)	Total office employment (%)	Number of establishments	Establishments (%)	Mean size
Primary industry	2·7	0·41	29	0·09	93·5
Food, drink and tobacco	5·5	0·83	104	0·32	52·5
Chemicals and allied industries	34·1	5·19	331	1·04	102·9
Metals and other metal goods	5·0	0·76	197	0·61	25·3
Engineering	23·6	3·61	595	1·87	39·7
Textiles, leather and clothing	5·8	0·88	751	2·36	7·7
Other manufacturing	6·5	0·98	350	1·10	18·4
Paper, printing and publishing	34·2	5·20	1138	3·58	30·0
Construction	17·8	2·71	599	1·88	29·7
Gas, electricity and water	9·4	1·43	57	0·17	164·5
Transport and communications	56·4	8·59	1423	4·47	39·6
Wholesale distribution	31·4	4·78	2823	8·88	11·1
Retail distribution	19·0	2·89	4390	13·81	4·3
Commodity dealing	31·4	4·79	2469	7·77	12·7
Insurance	70·3	10·72	1093	3·43	64·2
Banking	67·4	10·27	940	2·94	71·6
Other finance	40·1	6·11	1846	5·80	21·7
Professional and scientific services	76·0	11·59	4241	13·34	17·9
Business services	47·6	7·26	2367	7·44	20·1
Societies and associations	29·2	4·45	1487	4·63	19·6
Personal services	2·4	0·36	919	2·89	2·89
Entertainment	34·6	5·27	3423	10·77	10·1
Miscellaneous offices	5·5	0·84	5519	0·63	27·4

Examination of Table 9 suggests that there are some differences between sectors in the size distribution of establishments. The highest proportion of small establishments are to be found in retail distribution, personal services and entertainment; in each of these cases, office workers represent a small proportion of total employment. Wholesaling (mean size 11·1), commodity dealing (mean size 12·7), professional and scientific services (mean size 17·9), business services (mean size 20·1) and societies and associations (mean size 19·6) are all dominated by characteristically small establishments. In wholesale distribution (where many of the offices are associated with warehouses) 78·7% of the establishments employ less than 10 office workers. In like manner, in professional and business services, and societies and associations, 58·9%. 68·1% and 61·0% respectively of all establishments are in the under-10 category. In contrast, in the manufacturing sectors, establishments are on the average larger, especially in chemicals (mean size 102·9), where 65·9% of the employment (or 22,438 persons) work in establishments with a staff of over 250. An exception to this general rule concerning the manufacturing sectors is in textiles and clothing, where the mean size is only 7·7. In terms of size distribution, the insurance and banking sectors are akin to manufacturing, with a high proportion of employment in large establishments. The average employment in banking establishments is 71·6 persons and insurance 54·2, both with approximately half their total employment in units with over 250 staff.

A significant feature of the OSRP data is that it permits disaggregation of these broad employment categories — within which there can be considerable variations — into the more and more homogeneous three-and four-digit categories. For instance, within the chemicals and allied industries sector, 17,000 are employed in 18 office establishments of oil companies each with more than 250 office workers. Within paper, printing and publishing, 11,000 are employed in book publishing, but 192 of the 394 establishments in this category employ less than 10 office workers. Within transport and distribution, 17,000 are employed in shipping and forwarding agencies, again predominantly in small establishments. A further 17,000 office workers can be found in export and import merchants. In insurance, one-third of the employment is in specialist insurance like in insurance brokers and under-writing and the remainder in large insurance companies. In other finance, 16,000 are employed in stockbroking and 14,000 in property. Within professional services, 10,000 are employed in consulting engineers offices and 7000 in architects offices, while 20,000 in business services are employed in advertising and public promotions.

As an example of the distribution of employment by size of establishment within a sector, total employment in the other finance sector is disaggregated to the three-and four-digit levels in Appendix B. This appendix indicates the importance of different activities within a sector and reveals that considerable variation in the distribution of employment between size groups can be concealed by a high level of aggregation. For example, stockbroking and jobbing has 41% of the employment in the sector, the bulk of which is in the size range 51 – 100. The next largest activity — estate agents, surveyors and valuers — with 24% of employment in the sector, is dominated by small establishments. In complete contrast nearly one-third of the employment in building societies is in establishments with over 250 persons.

Space precludes the complete presentation of the employment structure of other office sectors. However, the significant feature of such a tabulation would be the very diversified employment structure of Central London, with 113 out of the 117 non-retailing four-digit categories containing more than 1000 office workers. We shall now move on to describe the distribution of this employment within Central London.

CHAPTER 2

The Localisation of Office Employment within Central London

INTRODUCTION

This chapter examines the extent to which different types of office employment are concentrated in particular parts of the Central Area and which types are more widely dispersed. The fact that certain activities are attracted to specific localities could in part reflect functional linkages with firms located in the same areas. However, before such spatial relationships — which are the focus of the next chapter — can be considered, it is essential to describe the location of each type of employment in turn.

A number of studies have been made of location patterns within large metropolitan centres, and these have used a variety of methods of analysis. Morgan in London (Morgan, 1961), Rannells in Philadelphia (Rannells, 1956), Davies in Capetown (Davies, 1965), Shachar in Tel Aviv (Shachar, 1967) and Alexander in Melbourne (Alexander, 1972) have all demonstrated how certain kinds of establishments tended to be grouped in particular parts of the city. The nature of these groupings has been demonstrated by direct mapping, concentration indices, delimitation of clusters on the ground and geo-statistical techniques. With the exception of Alexander's survey, each of the approaches was essentially univariate, describing the characteristics of each activity in turn. Comparisons between univariate measures were made by inspection or, as attempted by Davies, by overlapping clusters defined for different activities. Although of considerable interest, there are obvious limitations to the number of interrelationships that can be handled by such comparisons. Therefore, for logistic reasons as well as data limitations, these investigations were restricted to a very coarse classification of establishments. But as Davies himself points out, the typical business cluster in the city centre is characterised not by a single category of establishment but rather by a diversity of different businesses each deriving external economies from the other. The recognition of critical groupings therefore requires a detailed classification of nature of business of each establishment and a multivariate technique for distinguishing between all possible interrelationships. In this study we have been able to make use of employment data on 196 different types of offices and to compare the distribution of all possible pairs of activity, using the product moment correlation coefficient as a measure of similarity. Cluster analysis and component analysis has been used to identify sets of offices with similar patterns of location. The analysis of localisation presented in this chapter is a necessary prelude to the measurement of spatial association since one of the principal reasons for localisation could be involvement in a business cluster.

MEASURES OF CONCENTRATION

Three different indices of concentration have been used — the coefficient of localisation,

129

an index of concentration based on the Lorenz curve and the relative standard distance. Each measures different facets of the distribution. The coefficient of localisation is a measure of the concentration of employment in a particular area relative to all employment (Isard, 1960). Each grid cell's percentage share of employment in a particular category is subtracted from its percentage share of all office employment. The sum of the positive differences divided by 100 gives an index where 1·0 represents the maximum concentration (i.e. all employment in one cell) and 0·0 indicates complete dispersion (i.e. each cell with the same share of employment in the category has total employment). The Lorenz-curve index is a better measure of absolute concentration than the coefficient of localisation and does not rely on comparisons with a total employment base. This index is derived from a comparison of the cumulative proportion of employment in a particular category with the cumulative proportion of grid cells. In an even distribution, 25% of employment would be in 25% of the grid cells, 50% in 50% of the cells, and so on. A variety of indices to measure deviation from uniformity has been suggested; that used by Tress in the measurement of industrial diversification has been adopted here (Tress, 1938). To derive the index, the number of grid cells are ranked according to employment in the category in question and the employment figures cumulated to give a crude index of concentration — the higher the cumulative total the greater the concentration. To produce the index, the number of grid cells times 100 is subtracted from the cumulative total and the result is then divided by the number of grid cells times 50. An index of 0·0 therefore describes an even distribution.

Both of these indices are essentially non-spatial; they do not consider the geographical location of each unit of employment. This is achieved by a further index — the standard distance (Bachi, 1962; Neft, 1966; Shachar, 1967). Just as the standard deviation indicates the dispersion of a non-spatial distribution about its mean, so the standard distance considers the geographical dispersion of employment about the mean centre or centre of gravity of the distribution. Employment in each category is assumed to be located in the centre of each grid cell whose location is given by unique X and Y coordinates. Both X and Y values are weighted by the employment located at each point and the mean X and mean Y values calculated together with the variance in both directions. The intersection of mean X and mean Y locates the centre of gravity. The standard distance of the distribution about the centre is given by the square root of the sum of the variances along X and Y axes divided by the total employment in that category. This crude measure of standard distance for each employment group can be converted into a relative index by dividing it by the standard distance for all office employment. This will not necessarily be greater than that for the category in question, so indices greater than one are possible. Because distributions may consist of two distinct concentrations at different extremes of the Central Area, the mean centre will be located between the two and the standard distance about this centre will be high.*

In Table 10 the three indices have been used to rank the two-digit sectors in descending order of concentration. The divisions represent first, second, third and fourth quartiles of the distribution of each index. For this and all subsequent analyses, retail distribution, personal services and entertainment have been excluded from the data.

---

*In computing the standard distance, the square of differences about the mean centre are considered; this value is therefore particularly sensitive to employment located at the edge of the study area. A less-sensitive measure of dispersion would be that about the median centre or point that is least absolute distance from all employment. Unfortunately the identification of this point is extremely difficult.

TABLE 10. *Measures of localisation of Office Employment within Central London for Two-digit Sectors*

Coefficient of localisation.		Lorenz curve		Standard distance	
Highly concentrated		Highly concentrated		Highly concentrated	
1. PRI	0·848	1. PRI	0·964	1. INS	0·725
2. GEW	0·787	2. GEW	0·911	2. PPP	0·726
3. ENG	0·671	3. INS	0·886	3. BNK	0·757
4. CLT	0·665	4. BNK	0·884	4. CLT	0·765
5. MET	0·650	5. CLT	0·880	5. PRI	0·788
Moderately concentrated		Moderately concentrated		Moderately concentrated	
6. FDT	0·642	6. ENG	0·869	6. ENG	0·799
7. OMF	0·594	7. MET	0·864	7. BUS	0·850
8. CME	0·569	8. FDT	0·854	8. SOC	0·875
9. CON	0·521	9. MIS	0·850	9. COM	0·884
10. MIS	0·508	10. CHE	0·828	10. OMF	0·901
Moderately dispersed		Moderately dispersed		Moderately dispersed	
11. TRN	0·497	11. FIN	0·809	11. MET	0·922
12. PPP	0·490	12. OMF	0·808	12. GEW	0·911
13. SOC	0·467	13. TRN	0·791	13. WHS	0·924
14. BNK	0·466	14. PPP	0·775	14. CHE	0·925
15. IWS	0·426	15. COM	0·764	15. PRF	0·955
Highly dispersed		Highly dispersed		Highly dispersed	
16. BUS	0·411	16. BUS	0·717	16. FIN	0·971
17. FIN	0·389	17. CON	0·680	17. FDT	1·00
18. COM	0·335	18. WHS	0·659	18. MIS	1·01
19. WHS	0·334	19. PRF	0·655	19. CON	1·10
20. PRF	0·273	20. SOC	0·650	20. TRN	1·13

Key to codes for two-digit sectors

PRI	Primary industry	TRN	Transport and communications
FDT	Food, drink and tobacco	WHS	Wholesale distribution
CHE	Chemicals	COM	Commodity dealing
MET	Metals and other metal goods	INS	Insurance
ENG	Engineering	BNK	Banking
CLT	Clothing, leather and textiles	FIN	Other finance
OMF	Other manufacturing	PRF	Professional and scientific services
PPP	Paper, printing and publishing	BUS	Business services
CON	Construction	SOC	Societies and associations
GEW	Gas, electricity and water	MIS	Miscellaneous offices

According to the coefficient of localisation, industrial categories display the highest degree of concentration. The pure office functions all have moderate or high levels of dispersion, with professional and scientific services being the most dispersed group. Surprisingly, the financial categories also display moderate or high levels of dispersion. This is because these categories are relatively large employers and so tend to dominate the employment structure wherever they are located. This picture is reversed, however, when the concentration index is used; this reflects the absolute concentration of employment in insurance and banking and so places these two categories in the first quartile of ranked indices. Societies and associations and businesses and professional services all rank on these index as highly dispersed. Finally, when account is taken of the geographical disposition of employment in the standard distance indices, insurance and banking again rank as highly concentrated. Paper, printing and publishing also move into the upper quartile, while some of the industrial categories move down the ranking. This is largely a function of the multi-clustered nature of these distributions which leads to high standard distances.

Although important, many of these differences between employment sectors ignore significant differences within the sectors both at the three- and four-digit levels. For instance, while stockbroking and jobbing within the other finance sector is highly concentrated (CL = 0·743, SD = 0·205), most other categories (e.g. property, CL = 0·327, SD = 1·50) are highly dispersed, so giving an overall high level of dispersion for the group as a whole. Three- and four-digit measures of concentration for the other finance sector are given as examples of such within group variations in Table 11.

TABLE 11. *Measures of Localisation for Employment Categories within a Sector:*
Other Finance

Sector	Coefficient of localisation	Lorenz curve	Standard distance
Stockbroking and jobbing	0·743 (1)	0·982 (1)	0·205 (1)
Building societies	0·596 (4)	0·892 (3)	1·021 (4)
Investment and credit banks	0·685 (3)	0·949 (2)	0·732 (2)
Other finance	0·487 (4)	0·890 (3)	0·985 (4)
Property companies	0·434 (4)	0·792 (4)	1·150 (4)
Estate agents, surveyors and valuers	0·404 (4)	0·727 (4)	0·909 (4)
All other finance	0·384 (4)	0·809 (2)	0·971 (4)

Note: Figures in brackets refer to quartile numbers based on the ranking of all four-digit categories on each index (1 = most concentrated quartile).

AREAS OF LOCALISATION

A simple summary measure of employment in each of the two-digit employment sectors is provided by the location of its mean centre. In Fig. 3 each centroid is located by a circle proportional to the relative standard distance in quartile units. The location of the mean centres can be used to divide the employment sectors into four basic groups. Firstly, there are those sectors with centroids well to the east of that for all office employment; these are insurance, banking, finance and transport, which all have dominant concentrations of employment in the City. Secondly, a small group of sectors just to the east of the overall centre, namely paper, printing and publishing, wholesaling, gas, electricity and water, and food, drink and tobacco. Employment in these sectors has its concentration in the western part of the City and the middle part of the Central Area, including the Covent Garden area. From those sectors to the west of the overall centre, two further groups can be distinguished; firstly, to the south and west, and, secondly, those to the north and west of the centre for all employment. In the first group come societies, other manufacturing, construction, metal, chemicals and miscellaneous offices, with primary industry as a marked outlier to the groups;

all these have a principal weight of employment in Victoria and Westminster. In the second group comes clothing, engineering, business services and professional services, which each have a principal concentration of employment in the West End and Bloomsbury.

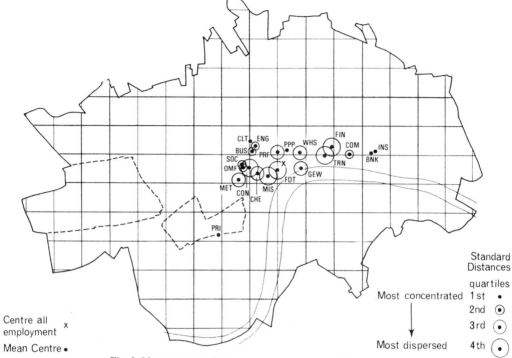

Fig. 3. Mean centres of office employment (two-digit sectors).

As noted earlier, the location of the mean centre is very sensitive to values at the extremes of the distribution and could be located in areas with no employment in that particular category. So Fig. 3 should be seen in the context of the specific areas of localisation that influence the position of the mean centre. A convenient way of depicting such areas with specific concentrations is through maps of location quotients. The location quotient is related to the coefficient of localisation in the sense that each grid square's percentage share of employment in a particular category is divided by its percentage share of all employment. An index of 1·0 indicates equal shares and that over 1·0 indicates a specific concentration. Because the index is based on relative shares, this implies that an area with a small amount of total employment may have a very high location quotient for a particular activity even though the absolute amount of employment involved may be very small.

It is not possible to reproduce location quotient maps for all the sectors. Again, other finance may be taken as an example. This sector is dominated by employment in stockbroking, and this is highly concentrated in the City. Outside the City there is a widespread distribution of employment in this sector. Just as there are variations within the sector in the size of distribution of establishments, so there are variations in location within the centre. This is indicated in Fig. 4 by the centres of gravity for employment in each of the four-digit categories that make up the sector. Although the overall centre of employment in the sector falls somewhere near St. Pauls, there is a wide scatter of different financial activities about this centre with, for example, the weight of building society employment falling in the West

End, north of Oxford Street, and property-owning centred near Charing Cross.

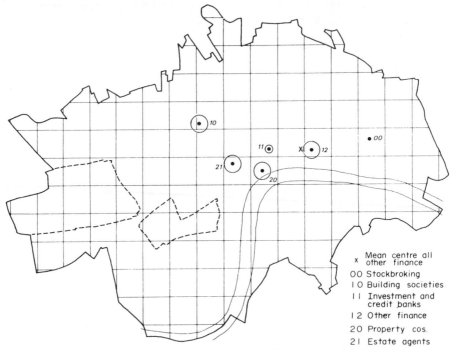

Fig. 4. Mean centres of employment categories within a sector: other finance.

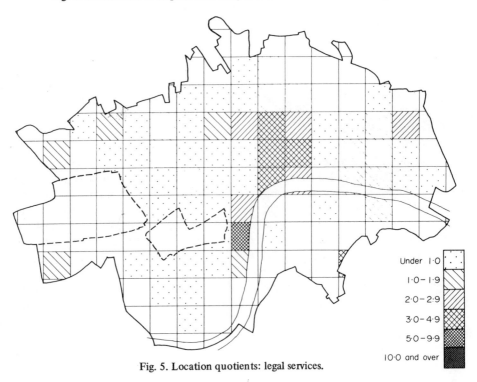

Fig. 5. Location quotients: legal services.

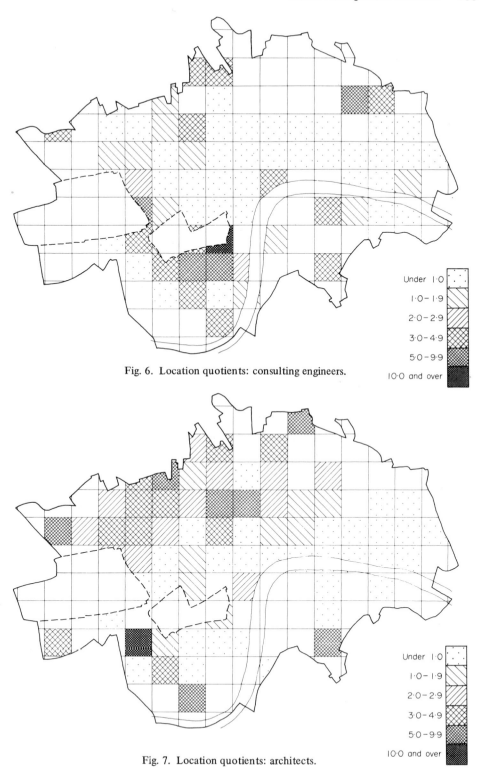

Fig. 6. Location quotients: consulting engineers.

Fig. 7. Location quotients: architects.

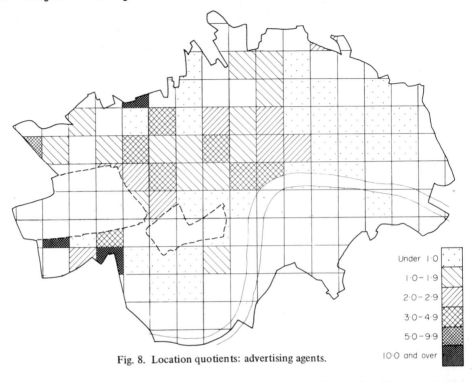

Under 1·0
1·0 – 1·9
2·0 – 2·9
3·0 – 4·9
5·0 – 9·9
10·0 and over

Fig. 8. Location quotients: advertising agents.

Specific areas of localisation can be identified within the professional and business services sector although no areas of concentration can be identified for the sector as a whole. Legal services are highly localised around the Law Court (Fig. 5), consulting engineers in Victoria (Fig. 6), architects in fashionable areas like Bloomsbury, Belgravia and the Portman Estate (Fig. 7), and advertising along Fleet Street and in the West End (Fig. 8). Nevertheless, these maps of location quotients and the measures of concentration indicate that the areas of localisation are far less pronounced than has sometimes been assumed (Morgan, 1961). When a time perspective is introduced there is clear evidence that these concentrations are declining. For example, Table 12 indicates that the point distribution of publishers' offices and advertising agencies over the period 1918-66 (recorded from Post Office directories) reveals a continuous deconcentration (Goddard, 1967). Such trends could be indicative of the relaxing of locational ties with the introduction of more advanced forms of interpersonal communication.

TABLE 12: *Changes in the Localisation of Publishers' Offices and Advertising Agents within Central London, 1918–1966*

Sector	1918	1938	1951	1966
Publishers	0·737	0·686	0·605	0·596
Advertising agencies	0·803	0·722	0·686	0·671

Note: The data are the number of establishments per 500 m grid square.
The index measures the amount of deviation from an even distribution.
Where the index = 1.0 each square would have an equal share of the total number of establishments.

THE EMPLOYMENT STRUCTURE OF SUB-AREAS

One of the chief disadvantages of the location quotient is that it does not take account of absolute amounts of employment. This difficulty can be overcome by a modified index of 'surplus workers' (Matilla and Thompson, 1955):

$$S_j = e_i - \frac{e_t}{E_t} \cdot E_i$$

where S_j is the total number of surplus workers in sector i in the grid cell j, e_i the employment in sector i in grid cell j, E_i the total employment in sector i in Central London, e_t tht total employment in grid cell j, and E_t the total employment in Central London.

This formula has been used to determine the absolute numbers of workers in each two-digit sector in each grid cell over and above those that would be expected on a *pro-rata* basis given that cell's share of all office employment. Clearly, some areas will have employment deficits in particular sectors and surpluses in others.

In order to provide a comprehensive picture of employment localisation within each cell, the number of surplus workers in each sector have been expressed as a percentage of the total number of surplus workers for that area and the percentages ranked in descending order.

The leading rank percentages have been mapped in Fig. 9 reading in order from the top left of the cell to the bottom right.

Obviously some areas will be dominated by a few sectors and others will have their total number of surplus workers divided between a large number of different sectors. In order to determine how many sectors significantly characterise the structure of each grid square, the percentage distribution of surplus workers has been compared with a number of 'model' situations (Weaver, 1955). In a model-one sector economic structure, 100% of the surplus workers would be in one sector; in a model-two sector structure, 50% would be in one sector, 50% in another, and so on. The sum of the squared differences of the actual percentage distribution of surplus workers from each of the possible model situations (1–20 sectors) are computed and the percentage distribution which gives the least deviation from the model situation is mapped. Thus if a particular cell has eight sectors with surplus workers and a five-sector model (20% in each sector) gives the lowest deviation, the first five sectors are used in the classification and the remainder ignored.

Using this classification procedure means that the number of different sectors characterising each area can be used as an indicator of the degree of diversity of the employment structure. Such an approach is an alternative to more usual indices of diversification, making it possible to identify the activities that contribute towards diversification or specialisation. Figure 9 clearly reveals the diversified economic structure of the West End with 8–10 sectors characterising each cell. Moving out from the West End, the level of specialisation increases in all directions.

Taking a transect from the western to the eastern side of the Central Area illustrates the changing degree of localisation as measured by the total number of surplus workers, the changing economic structure and the degree of diversification. The total number of surplus workers increases in the West End, and this is divided between a large number of sectors. These are headed by business and professional services, with clothing also ranking high. Moving to Soho and Covent Garden, the total concentration of employment drops, and paper, printing and publishing, together with wholesaling, moves into the economic structure, with professional and business services. Along Kingsway, engineering, finance and insurance enter into the structure, and the degree of diversification decreases. Along Fleet

c

Street, publishing moves into a leading position. Towards the central part of the City the total concentration of employment rapidly increases with banking, insurance and finance gradually taking up a leading position in the economic structure, until in the grid square containing the Bank of England these three sectors are completely dominant in a massive concentration of employment. Finally, in the eastern part of the City, the employment structure remains equally specialised but with transport moving into a dominant position.

In the West End outside Mayfair the employment structure becomes less diversified but is still dominated by business and professional services. Societies and associations also enter the picture, especially in Bloomsbury, where they are also found in conjunction with engineering and construction in a moderately diversified economic structure (4—6 sectors). A highly diversified structure can be found in the St. James area, but with transport, insurance, banking and finance frequently leading business and professional services. This area may therefore be regarded as a secondary financial and trading district after the City proper. In Victoria and Westminster there are moderate levels of diversification with industrial sectors, including primary industry, metals, chemicals and construction ranking high along with professional and business services and societies and associations. In Belgravia and Knightsbridge, professional services, societies and associations dominate a highly specialised economic structure.

South of the river, the South Bank is dominated by chemicals; further east, construction is important, giving this area affinities with Victoria and Westminster. Immediately south of the Fleet Street publishing area, around Blackfriars Bridge, paper and printing dominates a highly specialised economic structure. Around London Bridge Station the pattern of employment bears affinities with that to the north of the river, namely commodity trading, wholesaling and insurance. Thus the boroughs of Southwark and Lambeth, while not having remarkedly high levels of employment, clearly contain a number of office activities that can be related to the series of office areas on the other side of the river. To some extent a similar situation exists to the north of the City into which a number of the sectors dominant in the core of the area have extended. Thus, paper, printing and publishing, dominate the economic base of grid cells north-west from Fleet Street, along the line of King's Cross Road, while insurance, banking and finance extend northwards from the Bank of England along the line of Moorgate, and transport and insurance northwards along the line of Bishopsgate. In all of these areas to the north of the City, wholesaling also ranks high in the economic structure.

In summary, a picture emerges of a complex pattern of the spatial variation of economic structure from highly specialised to highly diversified areas. In the core of the City of London it is possible to identify a number of key areas where one or two employment sectors dominate; elsewhere, no such clear differentiation is apparent. Rather, in moving from one part of the centre to another the mix of activities changes in relative importance with different activities being added to a basic mix of business and professional services, and with these additional activities only occasionally occupying a leading position. Thus publishing ranks high in the western part of the City of London and in Covent Garden, engineering in the Aldwych-Kingsway area, clothing in Soho, insurance, banking, finance and transport in St. James, construction and chemicals, societies and associations in Victoria, and engineering and societies in Bloomsbury and the Tottenham Court Road area. Outside the City it is therefore difficult to talk of clearly distinguishable office districts dominated by a few activities, or, for that matter, in terms of characteristic mixtures of a large number of activities.

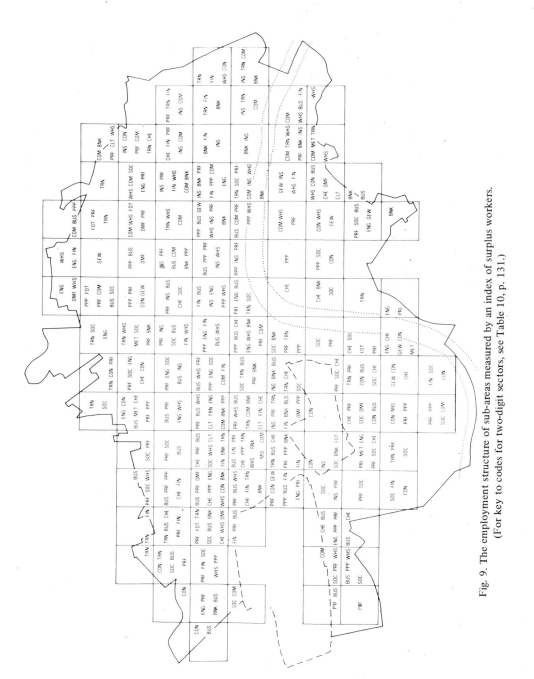

Fig. 9. The employment structure of sub-areas measured by an index of surplus workers. (For key to codes for two-digit sectors, see Table 10, p. 131.)

CHAPTER 3

Spatial Linkages of Office Employment

THE MEASUREMENT OF SPATIAL ASSOCIATION

In the last chapter it was observed that only a limited number of the two-digit employment sectors showed distinctive patterns of localisation within particular parts of Central
London. This is not to imply that it is only the highly localised sectors that are significantly
associated with other activities. In addition to an office cluster in which a number of
activities might have both spatial and functional relationships, linked activities may also
show similar patterns of dispersal throughout the Central Area. Also, the broad two-digit
classification necessarily adopted for the map analysis might conceal significant associations
within an office sector. In this chapter, similarities in the patterns of spatial variation of
office employment at the three- and four-digit levels will be examined using correlation
analysis and office clusters identified through cluster analysis and component analysis.

A number of features of correlation analysis as a measure of spatial association should be
stressed. First, the measures of association apply only to the particular system of areal units
that form the observations for the comparison of the employment variables. Secondly, the
coefficients are only a measure of within-cell associations (Duncan *et al.*, 1961;
McCarty *et al.*, 1956). In a partial attempt to assess the effect of different systems of
aggregation on the measures of association, the analysis was carried out with two completely
different sets of units — namely 112 grid squares and 61 traffic zones. Although higher
coefficients result from the use of larger units, the overall pattern of association as
indicated by components analyses were basically similar. Unfortunately it was not possible
to examine spatial association at a more disaggregated level than the 112 grid squares.
Below this, the next unit of measurement that was available was the street block, of which
there are many thousands in Central London. However, it can be argued that many of the
spatial linkages that are of significance occur within the 500-m squares that have been the
basis for much of this analysis.

As the preceding analysis has shown, many of the three- and four-digit employment
distributions were highly localised, with a large proportion of employment concentrated in
a limited number of grid squares. In statistical terms, this gives highly skewed frequency
distribution. A high correlation between two employment categories may therefore be due
to the absence of both from a large number of grid cells and their presence in the same
limited number of cells. This basic facet of reality creates a non-normality in many of the
frequency distributions which prevents the inferential interpretation of the correlation
coefficients. It does not, however, inhibit the use of the coefficients as a descriptive index.
Transformation of the data to meet the normality assumption would only destroy part of
the basic reality.

THE PATTERN OF WITHIN- AND BETWEEN-SECTOR CORRELATIONS

Because correlation analysis was carried out at two levels of sectoral aggregation, relationships within a two-digit sector (between the component four-digit activities) can be isolated from relationships between three-digit groupings in different sectors. Appendix C indicates that there are a few strong associations within or between the various manufacturing sectors. Textiles, leather and clothing are exceptions, with a complex pattern of association within the sector, though with few connections outside. Food industries show an expected association with various aspects of wholesale distribution. Publishing is associated with business services like advertising. Transport and communication activities are strongly associated with many aspects of trading, including commodity dealing and insurance underwriting. Insurance is also associated with banking, which is in turn linked particularly with stockbroking and accounting.

There are often differences in patterns of spatial association within a sector. Insurance is a particularly interesting example as can be seen from the full within-group correlation matrix shown in Table 13. Thus life insurance has a relatively weak association with risk insurance (principally fire, marine and casualty insurance, insurance broking, underwriting, re-insurance and insurance adjusting). In terms of external connections, life insurance is more strongly associated with banking and finance and casualty insurance than with shipping and commodity dealing.

TABLE 13. *Within-sector Correlations: Insurance*

Sector	Within-group correlations					
	1500	1501	1502	1510	1511	1512
1500 Life insurance companies	1·0000					
1501 Fire, marine and other casualty insurance	0·4029	1·0000				
1502 Life and casualty insurance combined	0·4847	0·4708	1·0000			
1510 Insurance brokers	0·3290	0·8451	0·3005	1·0000		
1511 Underwriters and underwriters agents	0·3085	0·7215	0·2237	0·7696	1·0000	
1512 Other insurance – re-insurance, insurance adjusting, etc.	0·3031	0·7559	0·2295	0·7837	0·9218	1·0000

In broad terms, a number of basic patterns can be identified. Firstly, a limited number of employment categories reveal strong associations only with other categories in the same sector and few links with other sectors (e.g. in textiles). Secondly, there are certain categories with significant links with other activities in the same sector and also with other sectors (e.g. in transport and communication). Thirdly, there are some categories that only have associations outside the sector (e.g. in food, drink and tobacco). Finally, there are large numbers of categories with no significant associations at all (e.g. in chemicals).

CLUSTER ANALYSIS

Cluster analysis can be used to unravel this complex pattern of interrelationships. This involves searching the four-digit correlation matrix for the two most highly correlated employment categories and combining these into a new group (Parks, 1966). The number of activities is therefore reduced by one; correlations of this new group with all other single categories are then computed and the reduced correlation matrix searched for the next most highly correlated pair, and these are likewise combined into a group. The process is repeated until all categories are combined into one group. This recomputation procedure has advantages over more simple forms of clustering like elementary linkage analysis (Johnston, 1968). The development of the grouping can be examined at different values for the correlation coefficient.

With a correlation cut off of 0·65, only four large clusters of employment categories can be distinguished. (Table 14). These are associated with:—

1. Commodity trading.
2. Shipping and marine insurance.
3. Banking and other finance.
4. Clothing and textiles.

TABLE 14. *Cluster Analysis: Membership of the Four Largest Groups*
(Four-digit Employment Categories)

Group 1: Commodity trading

Plantation house commodity dealers; grain merchants; other transport services; sugar and confectionery; other food products; agriculture, forestry and fishing; general wholesale merchants; tea and coffee merchants; property owning and developing companies; merchant banks.

Group 2: Shipping and marine insurance

Other insurance — re-insurance, insurance adjusting; underwriters and underwriters' agents; sea transport; postal services and telecommunications; insurance brokers; shipping and forwarding, freight broking, etc.; fire, marine and other casualty insurance; metal brokers and dealers.

Group 3: Banking and other finance

Other banks; bill discounting and foreign exchange; London clearing banks — other special departments; life and casualty insurance combined; stockbroking and jobbing; London clearing banks — head offices; other finance; accounting, auditing and bookkeeping; miscellaneous commodity brokers.

Group 4: Clothing and textiles

Footwear; dresses, lingerie; production and costing consultants; other clothing; clothing and footwear wholesaling; made-up textiles; drawing services, drawing office; scientific, surgical and photographic instruments, watches and clocks; women's tailoring and outerwear; direct-mail advertising circular services.

Note: Cluster inclusion limit $r = 0.55$.

A number of minor groups also appear: for instance, combining advertising services with publishing; public relations with advertising agencies; iron and steel with coal mining; shipbuilding with mechanical engineering; legal services with insurance companies; highway construction with bricks, pottery, glass and cement. At the 0·55 level a number of additional groups emerge, and other activities are also assigned to the basic clusters: for instance, estate agents, employment agencies and architects join public relations and advertising agencies in a group; radio and electrical goods join telegraph, telephone and telegraphic apparatus to form a new group, and consulting engineers join highway construction, bricks, pottery, glass and cement, and other mining and quarrying. At the 0·45 level, two of the basic groups — commodity trading plus transport services and insurance — join into one group. Finally, at the 0·35 level, all the basic financial and trading activities of the City combine into a group independent of the West End activities of which clothing and textiles form the core. Nevertheless, even at this general level there are a large number of activities that cannot be assigned to any group.

COMPONENTS ANALYSIS

Cluster analysis has been used to identify a small number of basic employment groups. But because it is essentially a stepwise hierarchical procedure, based simply on the comparison of absolute values of the correlation coefficient, the mis-allocation of an individual category to a particular group can upset all subsequent stages of the groupings. Components analysis followed by Varimax rotation of the leading components has therefore been applied to the correlation matrix in order to simultaneously identify basic clusters of employment variables. Examination of the eigenvalues is a guide to the number of basic patterns of employment variation and high component loadings indicate the employment categories associated with each pattern. The analysis has been carried out on the correlation matrix based on different levels of sectoral aggregation (three- and four-digit) and different systems of areal units (grid squares and traffic zones). The component structures that have emerged in all of these analyses are similar enough to support the contention that the regularities in the spatial distribution of employment types that has been identified do have some real significance. These results are also supported by the basic groupings identified through cluster analysis.

Table 15 indicates the similarities between the three-digit component analyses based on traffic zones and grid squares. Because the traffic zones are larger units and were designed to be as internally homogeneous as possible, component loadings and the levels of explained variance are higher than is the case with the grid-square analysis. Although a separate component associated with publishing cannot be identified in the grid-square analysis, the structure of the remaining factors is remarkably similar.

TABLE 15. *Components Analysis: Three-digit Employment Categories by Grid Square and Traffic Zones*

	Varimax rotated Component loadings	
	Grid square	Traffic zone
Component 1: Trading		
Transport services	0·89	−0·93
Commodity brokers	−0·85	−0·94
Other insurance	−0·44	−0·94
General wholesale merchants	−0·77	−0·83
Food wholesaling	−0·66	−0·74
Agriculture, forestry and fishing	−0·63	−0·83
Food manufacturers	−0·61	−0·69
Export and import merchants	−0·58	−0·67
Transport industries	−0·55	−0·68
Explained variance	16.8%	18.5%

TABLE 15 (continued)

	Varimax rotated Component loadings	
	Grid square	Traffic zone
Component 2: Clothing and business services		
Clothing and footwear wholesaling	−0·77	−0·74
Clothing and footwear manufacture	−0·74	−0·66
Management consultants	−0·72	−0·79
Drawing and photographic services	−0·64	−0·57
Drugs, chemicals and other non-food wholesaling	−0·62	−0·74
Advertising and public relations	−0·61	−0·59
Textile manufacture	−0·59	−0·69
Leather, leather goods and fur	−0·58	−0·58
Vehicle manufacture	−0·55	−0·57
Architects	−0·51	*
Timber and furniture	−0·50	*
Miscellaneous manufacturing	*	−0·53
Property	*	−0·53
Explained variance	9.9%	12.7%
Component 3: Banking and finance		
Stockbroking and jobbing	−0·88	0.89
Insurance companies	−0·87	0.81
Central banking	−0·86	0.86
Other banking	−0·80	0·86
Accounting	−0·78	0.94
Other finance	−0·76	0.76
Legal services	−0·72	0·60
Office services	*	0·63
Head offices, overseas companies	*	0·60
Explained variance	6·4%	6·8%
Component 4: Civil engineering		
Metal manufacturers	−0·63	*
Consulting engineers	−0·56	−0·78
Specialist contractors	−0·54	−0·54
Electrical engineering	−0·53	*
Architects	−0·53	−0·53
Mining and quarrying	−0·51	*
Bricks, pottery, glass and cement	*	−0·78
General construction and contracting	*	−0·60
Other specialist consultants		−0·65
Employers' trade associations	*	−0·82
Professional membership organizations	*	−0·59
Charities		−0·74
Explained variance	5·2%	7·5%
Component 5: Publishing		
Printing and publishing	*	−0·73
Paper, stationery and book wholesaling	*	−0·62
Drawing and photographic services	*	−0·51
Explained variance	*	5·3%
Total variance accounted by:		
Four components	37.3%	
Five components		50.8%

Note: Only loadings greater than ± 0.50 are listed. A separate publishing component could not be identified in the grid square analysis

TABLE 15 (continued)

Office employment in the three-digit sectors loading above ± 0.50 in the traffic zone analysis

Component	Employment (000's)	Central London total (%)
Trading	93.8	14.3
Clothing – business services	52.1	7.9
Banking and finance	155.9	23.7
Civil engineering	47.6	7.3
Publishing	38.8	5.9
TOTAL	388.2	59.1

The most important pattern is associated with the trading activities of the City, including transport services, risk insurance, commodity trading and export and import merchants. This component accounts for 18·5% of the overall spatial variation in employment by traffic zones and 16·8% by grid squares. Employment in the activities that go together to make up this cluster is highly localised in the eastern part of the City, as is shown by a plot of component scores (Fig. 10).

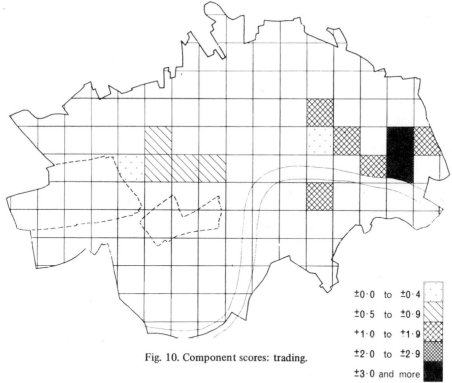

±0·0 to ±0·4
±0·5 to ±0·9
+1·0 to +1·9
±2·0 to ±2·9
±3·0 and more

Fig. 10. Component scores: trading.

A second basic pattern is associated with clothing and business services. In addition to a core of activities associated with the rag trade, this component includes a number of service categories localised in a similar part of the Central Area, like management consultants, advertising agencies and public relations consultants. This area of localisation is specified in

Fig. 11 as part of the West End together with a secondary area in the north of the City. In the traffic-zone analysis, some of these service activities are separately distinguished in component 5 as a small group associated with printing and publishing. Although publishing is found widely throughout the West End, a marked concentration of related activities can still be found in the Fleet Street area.

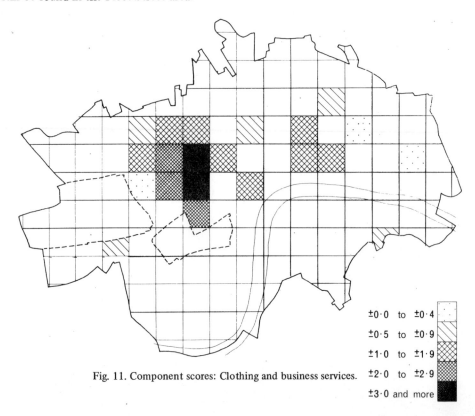

±0·0	to	±0·4
±0·5	to	±0·9
±1·0	to	±1·9
±2·0	to	±2·9
±3·0	and more	

Fig. 11. Component scores: Clothing and business services.

A third basic cluster includes activities related to civil engineering, including consulting engineers, general and specialised contracting, bricks, pottery, glass and cement and architects (Fig. 12). In the grid-square analysis, electrical engineering is also associated with this group. In addition, the group includes societies and associations, which are localised in a similar area. The map of component scores identifies Victoria and Bloomsbury as the two principal areas where this particular combination of activities can be found. The Aldwych-Kingsway area is of secondary importance due to a concentration of electrical-engineering employment.

A fourth component separates banking and finance from the trading activities in the City. This group includes central banking, insurance companies, stockbroking, accounting and legal services. The dominant area for these activities is in the central and northern part of the City, with a secondary area along High Holborn (Fig. 13). It seems that the basic distinction between the trading and financial functions of the City are clearly reproduced in spatial terms (Goddard, 1968; Dunning and Morgan, 1971). This is apparent at all scales of analysis. Using a four-digit classification of employment reveals separate trading and financial factors and indicates in detail how the various activities are assigned to different groups (Table 16). Table 16 also indicates the importance of variations within a three-digit sector with respect to spatial linkage patterns. Thus it is only sea transport and shipping and forwarding agents within the transport sector that are highly associated with the trading factor, and while insurance companies as a whole are not associated with this group, marine and casualty insurance companies are.

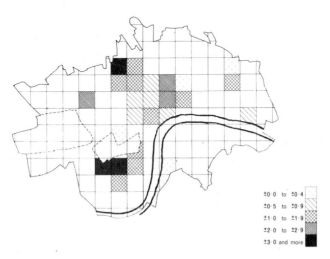

Fig. 12. Component scores: Civil engineering.

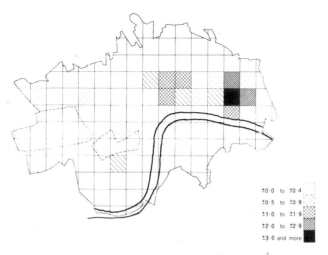

Fig. 13. Component scores: Banking and finance.

TABLE 16. *Components Analysis of Four-digit Employment Categories*
by Grid Squares (Trading and Financial Components)

Component 1: Trading

Grain merchants	−0·96
Plantation house commodity dealers	−0·93
Other transport services	−0·88
Insurance brokers	−0·85
Sugar and confectionery	−0·83
Shipping and forwarding, freight broking, etc.	−0·81
Property owning and developing companies	−0·78
Other food products	−0·77
General wholesale merchants	−0·77
Fire, marine and other casualty insurance	−0·71
Agriculture, forestry and fishing	−0·70
Metal brokers and dealers	−0·69
Underwriters and underwriters agents	−0·65
Sea transport	−0·64
Tea and coffee merchants	−0·64
Miscellaneous commodity brokers	−0·62
Grocery and provision wholesale	−0·60
Export and import merchants	−0·60
Other insurance − re-insurance, insurance adjusting	−0·56

(Explained variance = 8·37%)

Component 3: Banking and Finance

Other banks	−0·82
Stockbroking and jobbing	−0·81
London Clearing banks − other special departments	−0·81
Life and casualty insurance combined	−0·80
Accounting, auditing and bookkeeping	−0·75
Bill discounting and foreign exchange	−0·74
London Clearing banks − head offices	−0·73
Legal services	−0·72
Other finance	−0·71
Life insurance companies	−0·69
Typewriting, duplicating and photocopying	−0·57
Miscellaneous commodity brokers	−0·51

(Explained variance = 6·53%)

The main distinction between trading and financial activities was apparent from an earlier study of spatial linkages *within* the City of London. Here the observations were 216 street blocks and the variables 80 employment categories, some of which were similar to those used in the present study. Five basic factors were found to underline spatial variations of employment within the City (Table 17). The first of these was a trading factor remarkably similar in composition to the trading factor identified in the study of the wider area, including transport services and risk insurance. The financial factor identified in the Central London analysis can be divided into two, namely a 'financial core' factor including central banking and insurance, and a 'financial ring' factor including the investment side of finance, particularly stockbroking and jobbing. A publishing and professional services factor and a textile trading factor also emerged in this micro analysis of the City

Because components analysis forces out non-overlapping clusters, this analysis has identified five groupings of employment categories that in statistical terms are mutually independent. However, many of the areas of localisation that had been identified on the maps of component scores are geographically overlapping. Although there are core areas where particular types of employment are dominant, the activities of one sector are not completely excluded from the core area of the other. Also, in functional terms, while trading activities, for example, form a distinctive cluster of interlinked functions, these activities must draw to some extent upon the services provided by the cluster of activities forming the banking and financial set. In other words, rather than being independent, these basic groups are interrelated at a higher level.

TABLE 17. *Basic Factors Underlying the Spatial Variation of Employment within the City of London*

Primary variable	Factor loading	Primary variable	Factor loading
Factor 1. The trading factor		**Factor 3. Publishing & professional**	
General produce merchants	−0·65	services factor	
Transport services	−0·63	Printing & publishing of newspapers	
Grain dealers	−0·61	& periodicals	−0·60
Tea and coffee merchants	−0·60	Advertising & public relations	−0·59
Dealers in other plantation house		Other professional services—	
commodities	−0·58	consultancy	−0·58
Miscellaneous commodity dealers		Paper & board manufacturers	−0·45
	−0·55	Other business services	−0·41
Lloyds insurance brokers	−0·52	Wholesale distribution—paper,	
Food, drink and tobacco		stationery, books	−0·41
manufacturers	−0·17	Miscellaneous services	−0·37
Port and inland water transport	−0·47		
Wholesale distribution—grocery		**Factor 4. Textile trading and other**	
and provision	−0·47	**manufacturing factor**	
Rubber merchants	−0·47	Wholesale distribution—clothing &	
Shipping companies, airlines	−0·45	footwear	0·71
Other insurance brokers	−0·45	Leather, leather goods & fur	0·60
Other insurance—re-insurance	−0·45	Textile manufacturers	0·58
Shipbuilding	−0·42	Clothing & footwear manufacturers	
Wholesale distribution—tobacco	−0·39		0·51
Metal dealers	−0·39	Wooldealers	0·43
Import & export merchants	−0·38	Other manufacturing industries	0·43
Underwriters & underwriters'		Construction	0·43
agents	−0·38	Wholesale distribution—other	
Non-life insurance	−0·37	non-food goods	0·39
Factor 2. The financial 'ring' factor		**Factor 5. The financial core factor**	
Stockbrokers and jobbers	0·60	British Overseas Commonwealth	
Other finance—buildings		banks	0·74
societies, etc.	0·55	Scottish & Northern Irish banks	0·68
Other banks	0·53	Members of the Discount Market	0·68
Foreign banks	0·53	Life & non-life insurance companies	
Investment and unit trusts	0·52		0·50
Accountants	0·49	London Clearing banks—headquarters	
Finance Houses	0·48	offices	0·42
Mining companies	0·47	Non-life insurance	0·41
		Other banks	0·41
		Life insurance	0·34

To allow for interrelationships between basic clusters and the possibility of higher order groupings, one of the constraints on the proceeding components analysis, namely that the components should be statistically independent, has been relaxed in the rotational

procedure. Applying an oblique Promax rotation to the four-digit component analysis reveals that there is, indeed, a correlation between the trading factor and the finance factor of 0.385 and between the professional services and publishing factors of 0·281. For details of Promax rotation, see Hendrickson and White, 1964. The banking and trading factors are both inversely related to business services. Having allowed for this intercorrelation between components, it is possible to search for higher-order relations by abstracting new components from the inter-component correlation matrix. For this analysis, a total of ten components were subjected to a Promax rotation. From the 10 by 10 correlation matrix, three new higher-order-rotated components were extracted. These components are identified in terms of the original variables in Table 18.

TABLE 18. *Higher-order Components. Four-digit Employment Categories by Grid Square*

Component 1. The City: trading and finance

Metal brokers and dealers	−0·86
Insurance brokers	−0·79
Underwriters and underwriters' agents	−0·79
Fire, marine and other casualty insurance	−0·78
Shipping and forwarding, freight broking, etc.	−0·76
Property owning and developing companies	−0·75
Accounting, auditing and bookkeeping	−0·72
Other banks	−0·72
Grain merchants	−0·72
Bill discounting and foreign exchange	−0·71
Miscellaneous commodity brokers	−0·71
Other insurance−re-insurance, insurance adjusting	−0·69
Plantation house commodity dealers	−0·66
Export and import merchants	−0·66
Tea and coffee merchants	−0·66
Head offices of enterprises operating abroad	−0·65
General wholesale merchants	−0·63
Other finance	−0·63
Merchant banks	−0·61
London clearing banks − other special departments	−0·61
Sea transport	−0·60
Other transport services	−0·59
Life and casualty insurance combined	−0·54
Agriculture, forestry and fishing	−0·53
Sugar and confectionary	−0·53
Life insurance companies	−0·51
Postal services and telecommunications	−0·50
Grocery and provision wholesale	−0·49
Other food products	−0·48
Stockbroking and jobbing	−0·48
Legal services	−0·47

(Explained variance = 10·43%)

Component 2. The West End: Clothing, professional and business services

Clothing and footwear wholesaling	0·85
Fur	0·82
Footwear	0·81
Dresses, lingerie	0·80
Other clothing	0·76
Made-up textiles	0·75

TABLE 18 (continued)

Drawing services, drawing office	0·64
Production and costing consultants	0·63
Management consultants	0·63
Employment agencies	0·63
Other non-food goods wholesaling	0·62
Commercial photographic services	0·61
Textile manufacture	0·61
London Clearing banks – branches	0·58
Scientific, surgical and photographic instruments, watches and clocks	0·55
Women's tailoring and outwear	0·55
Vehicles	0·54
Public relations consultants	0·52
Advertising agencies	0·51
Air transport	0·49
Wool and fur dealers	0·48
Fruit and vegetables	0·45
Estate agents, surveyors and valuers	0·47
Marketing consultants and market research	0·44
Other business services	0·42

(Explained variance = 8·17%)

Component 3. Midtown: Publishing, professional and business services

Legal services	−0·69
Book publishing	−0·62
Architects	−0·59
Advertising services	−0·56
Typewriting and duplicating, photocopying	−0·54
Printing, engraving, lithographic work	−0·52
Other commercial and professional machinery and equipment	−0·47
Other specialist consultants	−0·47
Professional membership associations	−0·47
Advertising agencies	−0·46
Life insurance companies	−0·45
Paper, stationery and books wholesaling	−0·44
Publishing of daily and weekly newspapers	−0·44
Public relations consultant	−0·43
Diamond merchants	−0·43
Commercial photographic services	−0·42
Office machinery and equipment – supplies and service	−0·42
Calculating services	−0·40
Dairy products	−0·40
Shop and office fitting	−0·40

(Explained variance = 6.16%)
Total variance accounted for by three higher-order factors = 24·76%

The three higher-order components can be given clear functional and geographical interpretations. The first component combines the trading and financial activities of the City, which together set this area apart from the rest of Central London. The second component combines clothing and professional and business services localised in the West End. The third higher-order component combines publishing and professional and business services localised in the intermediate area between the City and the West End, extending from Fleet Street through Covent Garden to Bloomsbury. Activities localised in Westminster and Victoria do not contribute significantly to any of these higher-order groups. Nevertheless, in spatial terms there is a clear division of Central London into a number of distinctive office areas.

CONCLUSION

The fact that similar groupings of employment types emerge at all scales of analysis, both geographically and sectorally, is most encouraging. The basic set of activities that are involved – trading, finance and banking, printing and publishing, clothing and textiles, and civil engineering – must therefore represent a number of fundamental office complexes. However, it does seem that in spatial terms the bulk of office employment that makes up these complexes is highly localised in the City. It is here that office employment is most clearly organised into a number of identifiable office areas; elsewhere in Central London the spatial arrangement of office activities is far less structured.*

In terms of employment, the sectors that make up the non-City clusters are relatively unimportant in the overall economic structure of Central London. Together, the three-digit sectors that load above 0·5 on the non-City traffic zone components account for only 45% of Central London employment (Table 15). The more detailed four-digit analysis also makes clear that not all employment within a particular three-digit sector is spatially linked to a group. At this level of resolution an even smaller proportion of total Central London employment can be associated with basic office clusters. It would also be incorrect to assume that in spatial terms all employment at whatever level of analysis belongs to a particular office cluster. For example, a considerable proportion of life insurance employment can be found outside the City, even though this sector loads high on the financial factor.†

The analysis of spatial linkages raises all sorts of questions concerning the functional significance of office clusters – such as whether employment of the same kind as that located within a cluster can be regarded as functionally related to the cluster as a whole. But the basic issue is how far patterns of spatial association that have been identified in this analysis can be regarded as reflecting strong functional linkages, particularly in the form of information transmitted through personal contact. It is this question that is the focus of the survey of office communication described in Part II of this report.

*If the City had been excluded from this analysis, the City-type complexes might not have so clearly dominated the pattern of spatial linkages; it might then have been possible to identify some distinctive West End clusters.

†To assess the proportion of employment in a particular sector belonging to a cluster would require a multivariate classification of uniform office area in Central London. Unfortunately, the highly skewed nature of the scores of each grid square on each of the basic components makes an objective definition using multivariate grouping techniques impossible. The majority of the areas in Central London do not score significantly on any of the components and are therefore highly similar; they would combine into clusters long before the distinctive high scoring areas form any group.

PART II

Office Communications Patterns in Central London

CHAPTER 4

The Survey of Office Communications

INTRODUCTION

Part I of this report was primarily concerned with describing the office employment structure of Central London and the distribution of various types of office employment within the area. A number of distinctive patterns of localisation have been identified and a few clearly definable groups of employment categories have been isolated on the basis of similar geographical distributions. The objective of this second part of the study is, firstly, to assess how far these geographical groupings correspond to functionally linked office activities, and, secondly, to measure the strength of these linkages – i.e. how far spatial proximity is a necessary feature of functional linkage. In this analysis, information flows through personal contacts by telephone, and face-to-face meetings are taken as the indicator of functional relationship.

To achieve the first objective a large amount of survey data would be required on the volume of contact between firms in different office sectors. The second objective raises a number of fundamental questions about the nature of interpersonal communications and their role in office location, particularly concerning the substitutability between face-to-face contact and present and future systems of telecommunications. If large volumes of contact at present maintained at high cost by face-to-face meetings and therefore demanding a central location could be transferred to telecommunications, then one of the chief reasons for offices to remain in Central London could be undermined.

While the identification of office clusters might best be achieved by a relatively simple survey of the aggregate amount of contact between a large sample of firms, measuring the strength of these linkages requires that the characteristics of the contacts are examined in greater detail.

Pilot studies demonstrated that the only effective way of obtaining even aggregate figures of contacts was through the use of contact diaries in which each contact event is separately recorded. At the same time, it is fairly easy to obtain additional information on the characteristics of the contact. A decision was therefore made to examine in detail the communication patterns of a limited number of firms in different office sectors using diary techniques.

THE USE OF CONTACT DIARIES

Although the importance of face-to-face contact as a locational determinant has been repeatedly emphasised in studies of office-location decisions, only a few surveys have been made of the actual pattern of contacts between organisations and organisational units

153

D

(Thorngren, 1970; Tornqvist, 1970; Sahlberg, 1969; Hedberg, 1969). At a micro level, within organisations, the significance of communications between managers has been widely appreciated by behavioural scientists, and an increasing number of surveys have been made of actual contact patterns (e.g. Stewart, 1967). Experience gained in such surveys is clearly relevant to more macro-locational studies.

Two main methods of surveying communications have been used. The first involves respondents estimating the amount and type of communication and recording this information in a self-completion questionnaire. In the second, respondents record details of each contact as and when it occurs, either on a single line of a table or in a diary in which one sheet is used for each contact. These survey methods can be distinguished from time budgets or travel diaries in the sense that each contact is treated as a discrete event and no continuous record of the use of time is maintained (Anderson, 1971; Garrison and Worral, 1968)

Few evaluations have been made of the validity of such surveys, although one exercise is now under way at the Communications Study Group in London (Connell, 1972). The validity of the survey data depends on its relationship to the contacts that have actually occurred during the survey period. The issue of validity raises such questions as What proportion of the contacts have been recorded? Are certain types of contact underrecorded, or are certain types of individuals underrecording their contacts? And, finally, Are there disagreements between the respondents in recording the characteristics of the same contacts?

Very little is known about the second and third questions although there is some information about the proportion of contacts that are recorded and the inconsistencies between respondents. The most difficult types of survey to check in these respects and those which are mostly likely to produce unreliable data are surveys based on an estimation of the total amount of contact. Pilot work in this project showed that such questionnaires are extremely difficult to design, especially if a list of all likely contacts cannot be prepared in advance. A check-list of business sectors rather than individual firms creates problems of classification for the respondents, and if some weighting like frequency and mode of communication are required, the questionnaire becomes very cumbersome. In estimation it is also difficult to control the length of time to which the respondent refers. In any case, it is likely that the return will be dominated by repetitive or routine contacts which could be less significant than those taking place at lower frequency. These problems become inflated if one person is expected to complete a questionnaire giving average contact figures for a whole unit. Because contacts occur at the individual level there is a high degree of variability in contact pattern between individuals, and so gross estimates are likely to be meaningless.

Estimation procedures are most useful when the survey has been carefully controlled, and is principally concerned with communications between different parts of one large organisation. Such a situation prevailed in a recent survey of contacts in the British Civil Service (Elton *et al.,* 1970). The basic units of measurement were 'blocks of work'; all blocks of work relevant to each individual were clearly identified prior to the survey. Respondents were then asked to estimate their frequency of contact with other blocks of work covering a 3-month period.

The next level of detail is provided by questionnaires in which respondents are asked to record each contact on a single line as and when it occurs. Surveys by Hesseling and Graves have used this method (Hesseling, 1970; Graves 1972). Although they have not examined underrecording, these studies have demonstrated a high degree of inconsistency at the individual level between the characteristics of the same contact as recorded by different participants. One participant might record against a meeting with a particular person that he meets that person 'frequently', but the other person might record this as an 'infrequent' contact. At the micro level these differences in how individuals see the same contact give important guidelines to the researchers as to the real position of the individual within an organisation. However, when both ends of the communication link are not surveyed, it is impossible to check for such inconsistencies.

Most information on the characteristics of contacts can be obtained from a contact diary in which details of each contact are noted on separate contact record sheets. This method was first used in the study of internal communications by Weinshall who observed, over a 2-week period, only a 21% level of agreement between participants that a telephone call had actually occurred, and a 27% level of agreement that a face-to-face meeting had occurred. The level of agreement concerning the characteristics of the contact was 60% for telephone calls and for 44% face-to-face meetings (Weinshall, 1968).

This form of diary was first used in locational studies by Thorngren. Informants in a single decentralised office recorded details of external meetings and telephone calls on six randomly selected days. Checking the meeting data against a central register of persons entering and leaving the building revealed that 83% of all contacts were recorded (Thorngren, 1967). So for external contacts, which occur with lower frequency than internal contacts, more reliable data is produced. In a later survey of thirty-four government agencies due to be decentralised from Stockholm, Thorngren used a very long external contact record sheet, and this was completed for two separate 3-day periods. Checks were made at the level of each agency on both the number of contacts recorded between agencies and on the overall characteristics of both telephone and face-to-face meetings, and these revealed a consistency to within 1% (Thorngren, 1972). So when contacts are aggregated to the level of the organisation, inconsistencies noted by Hesseling, Graves and Weinshall at the individual level seem to cancel themselves out.

The validity of the contact data is also likely to be related to the length of time that the survey covers. Thorngren's pilot studies suggested that after a 3-day period the proportion of actual contacts that were recorded fell rapidly. For this reason, the present study was confined to a 3-day period. It included both external telephone calls and face-to-face meetings. Although telephone contacts do not require close proximity, if the questions of substitutability and the stretching of contact links was to be considered, the characteristics and volume of both forms of communication needed to be established. Furthermore, telephone calls are closely connected with past or future meetings, and in view of the limitation of a 3-day period, more frequently occurring telephone calls are likely to give a more complete picture of an individual's total contact network.

Because of the proven reliability of the single contact record sheet form adopted by Thorngren, a very similar diary was designed for this survey. An example of a meeting record sheet is given in Fig. 14. A different-coloured record sheet covering only the relevant questions was used for telephone calls. One sheet is completed after each contact. The record sheets were provided in a special folder which contained full instructions and further background information on the project, together with a short questionnaire to help in the classification of each respondent according to job type. In addition to the questions on the sectoral and geographical distribution of contacts, mode of travel and length of journey, a number of features of the contact themselves were recorded. These are fully discussed in Chapter 7.

MEETING RECORD

1 How long did the meeting last?

1 ☐   2-10 minutes
2 ☐   10-30 minutes
3 ☐   30-60 minutes
4 ☐   1-2 hours
5 ☐   more than 2 hours

2 Was the meeting arranged in advance?

1 ☐   Not pre-arranged at all
2 ☐   Arranged on the same day
3 ☐   Arranged the day before
4 ☐   Arranged 2-7 days in advance
5 ☐   Arranged more than 1 week in
          advance

3 Who initiated the meeting?

1 ☐   Myself/another person in my firm
2 ☐   Any person outside the firm or
          any other organization

4 How many people, apart from you, were at the meeting?

1 ☐   One other person
2 ☐   2-4 people
3 ☐   5-10 people
4 ☐   over 10 people

IF there was **only one** other person at the meeting:-

5 What is the work address of that person?

....

....

6 What is the nature of business of his firm?

....

....

IF there was **more than one** other person at the meeting, please complete the details overleaf

7 How often on average do you have a meeting with this person or particular set of people?

1 ☐   Daily
2 ☐   About once a week
3 ☐   About once a month
4 ☐   Occasionally
5 ☐   First contact

8 What was the main purpose of the meeting?

1 ☐   To give an order or instruction
2 ☐   To receive an order or instruction
3 ☐   To give advice
4 ☐   To receive advice
5 ☐   For bargaining
6 ☐   To give information
7 ☐   To receive information
8 ☐   To exchange information
9 ☐   For general discussion
10 ☐ Other (please specify)................
          ....

9 What was the range of subject matter discussed?

1 ☐   One specific subject
2 ☐   Several specific subjects
3 ☐   A wide range of general subjects

10 Was the meeting concerned with the purchase or sale of goods or services?

1 ☐   Directly concerned with
          purchases or sales
2 ☐   Indirectly concerned with
          purchases or sales
3 ☐   Not at all concerned with
          purchases or sales

IF the meeting took place outside your place of work:-

11 What is the address of the meeting place?

....

....

12 What was your principal method of transport from your office or previous meeting place?

1 ☐   Walk
2 ☐   Bus
3 ☐   Private car
4 ☐   Taxi
5 ☐   Underground
6 ☐   Train
7 ☐   Plane

13 How long did this journey take?

1 ☐   Less than 10 minutes
2 ☐   10-30 minutes
3 ☐   30-60 minutes
4 ☐   1-2 hours
5 ☐   More than 2 hours

Fig. 14. An example of a meeting record sheet.

SAMPLING PROCEDURES AND ORGANISATION OF THE SURVEY

A two-stage sampling procedure involving, first, the selection of firms and then individuals within firms, had to be adopted. The register of office establishments described in Part I was used to draw three samples of 300 offices, one initial list and two replacement lists. The probability of an establishment being selected was proportional to its size with the number of establishments drawn from each two-digit office sector set proportional to the total employment in the sector. This procedure was adopted because large establishments account for such a substantial proportion of total employment in central London (see Chapter 2). Large establishments are also likely to display a greater diversity of contact patterns.

A lengthy personal approach to firms was necessary in order to achieve co-operation. This consisted of an introductory letter, telephone calls for an appointment to explain the survey and, finally, a meeting with management representatives. This was often followed by a long delay before a decision was made by the firm to co-operate or not and before diaries were filled in and returned. It was therefore necessary to adopt a rolling programme of field work. Given the resources available it was impossible to have all of the diaries in different firms completed at the same time, even though this does have a number of advantages — such as insuring the data is available for analysis at a specific time and that firms do not delay the survey until a slack period. Better prior publicity can also be achieved with such a survey, but this may be counteracted by firms being unable to co-operate because the survey period coincides with a particularly difficult time for internal reasons.

Because of the nature of the rolling programme it is difficult to define a response rate. In the first instance it was only possible to approach 225 firms out of a target of 300. Towards the end of the survey period (February-September 1970) firms were selected to match up, with target, sector and size distributions. By the time the survey had to be wound up, businessmen from 72 firms had completed diaries, 22 firms who had agreed to co-operate had not completed diaries, 12 were still actively thinking about it, 9 appointments were pending and 33 approach letters had not been answered; 77 firms completely refused to co-operate (34% of the total approached). If the refusal rate for the outstanding firms had been the same as earlier, this would have amounted to a response rate of 54% (130 firms out of 225).

The second-stage sampling involved the selection of personnel within the establishment to complete a contact diary. It was decided to restrict the survey to contacts external to the *firm* in Central London, since these are most relevant to location.* If the sampled establishment was part of a larger organisational unit in Central London, the survey therefore had to be extended to all such units.

As little was known about what characteristics of individuals might be significant discriminators as to the amount and type of contact, a rigorous stratified sampling procedure was out of the question. Although job type is likely to be relevant, there is no widely adopted job classification system that could be used for the stratification of the sample. Clearly, the job of an individual is obviously related to the administrative unit in which he works, and it is these units that are likely to be the basic components involved in any decentralisation. An attempt was therefore made to place at least two diaries in every separately identifiable organisational unit within the firm in Central London. Although this placing was discussed with management by the field workers, the final distribution of diaries had to be left with the firm. Even though the survey excluded clerical grades, it was not always possible to get the desired number of returns. Usually a compromise had to be made between an ideally large sample or no sample at all. Other biases probably entered in the distribution stage, diaries in some instances being given to the busiest executives, while in others these were the people who deliberately avoided the survey. However, across the

---

*In some instances the definition of the 'firm' proved so difficult that in retrospect it would have been more appropriate to have used an establishment definition of external contacts — basically those outside the building.

whole sample of 705 completed diaries these differences probably cancel each other out. Obviously a more rigorous sampling procedure would have been desirable but was just impracticable.

TABLE 19. *Size and Sector Distribution of Firms Co-operating in the Survey of Office Communications*

Sector	Size groups				Sample (%)	No. of diaries	Percentage of diaries	Office employment (%)
	1−25	26−100	100+	Total				
Primary industry	−	1	−	1	1·4	1	0·1	0·4
Food, drink and tobacco	−	−	1	1	1·4	9	1·3	0·8
Chemicals and allied industries	−	3	4	7	9·7	135	19·1	5·2
Metals and other metal goods	1	−	−	1	1·4	1	0·1	0·8
Engineering	1	−	4	5	6·9	54	7·7	3·6
Other manufacturing	−	−	2	2	2·8	31	4·4	1·0
Printing, paper and publishing	1	−	1	2	2·8	24	3·4	5·2
Construction	−	2	1	3	4·2	26	3·7	2·7
Gas, electricity and water	−	−	2	2	2·8	19	2·7	1·4
Transport and communications	−	2	−	2	2·8	3	0·4	8·6
Wholesale distribution	−	1	1	2	2·7	5	0·7	4·8
Retail distribution	2	1	1	4	5·5	14	2·0	2·9
Commodity dealing	3	−	1	4	5·5	11	1·6	4·8
Insurance	−	3	3	6	8·3	44	6·2	10·7
Banking	−	2	4	6	8·3	113	16·0	10·3
Other finance	1	2	2	5	6·9	67	9·5	6·1
Professional and scientific services	1	1	2	4	5·5	44	6·2	11·6
Business services	1	1	4	6	8·3	49	7·0	7·3
Societies and associations	1	1	1	3	4·2	8	1·1	4·5
Entertainment	2	−	3	5	6·9	44	6·2	5·3
Miscellaneous offices	1	−	−	1	1·4	3	0·4	0·8
Total number of firms	15	20	37	72				
Percentage of sample in each size group	21	29	50					
Percentage of OSRP employment in each size group	23	27	50					

Because of the difficulties of controlling for the number of diaries actually completed within each firm, the distribution of diaries between each sector does not correspond very well with that of total office employment (Table 19). For example, textiles, leather and clothing, − a sector dominated by small establishments − is underrepresented. In contrast, the chemicals sector − containing the major oil companies − is greatly overrepresented.

This is because this sector is dominated by large establishments with a high probability of selection and also because several oil companies participated very actively in the survey and returned a large number of diaries. Banking is overrepresented for similar reasons. Transport, commodity dealing and professional services, all with an above-average share of employment in small establishments, are all underrepresented. Nevertheless, the overall size distribution of sampled establishments corresponds very well with the distribution of total employment.

CHAPTER 5

The Generation of Business Contacts

INTENSITY OF BUSINESS CONTACTS BY BUSINESS SECTOR

Because of variations in the number of respondents in each sector it is necessary to make comparisons on a standardised basis of contact per respondent. Altogether the 705 respondents in the survey recorded details of 5266 telephone contacts and 1954 meetings, an average of 10·0 contacts per head (7·4 telephone; 2·6 meetings) for a 3-day period. Generally speaking, the higher intensity of contact was recorded by individuals in financial sectors but only marginally so. The average contact intensity figure for the financial group was 7·9 telephone calls and 2·5 meetings per head, compared with 6·5 and 1·9 respectively for manufacturing sectors. Business and professional sectors record the same contact intensity as firms in the financial sectors. Examining those sectors with a sample size of more than 20 respondents reveals considerable variations in contact intensity (Table 20). For instance, the other finance sector has a higher intensity of telephone contacts than banking but a lower intensity of meetings. Over all the sectors there is a fair correspondence between contacts according to both means of communication. In other words, as the intensity of meetings increases, so likewise does the intensity of telephone calls, with a few sectors showing a clear preference for one medium rather than the other. This is indicative of the close connection between the two forms of communication.

INTENSITY OF CONTACT BY STATUS GROUP AND TYPE OF DEPARTMENT

The variations between sectors in intensity of contact could in part be explained by the differences in the occupational composition of the office labour force within different sectors, with manufacturing sectors having a lower proportion of clerical staff working in Central London than financial firms. Table 21, indeed, indicates that even within the managerial grades that have taken part in the survey there are considerable variations in contact intensity according to status level. Managing directors record on average 3·2 meetings compared with 1·3 meetings for executives. External telephone contacts drop to an average of 10·2 for managing directors to 6·5 for assistant managers, but rise again in the executive grades*

---

*These results compare very well with those obtained in the pilot study for the Civil Service (Elton *et al.,* 1970). In the Civil Service external meetings climb consistently with status but external telephone contacts and also paper flows, after a decline in volume from the under-secretary level, rise again rapidly in the lower executive grades. Both in the public and commercial sector this rise can'be attributed to a large volume of fairly routine work. There are also indications that middle grades are more involved in internal communications than higher or lower grades.

TABLE 20. *Intensity of Contact by Sector*

Manufacturing	Chemical	Engineering	Other manufacturing	Paper, printing and publishing	Construction	All manufacturing [a]
No. of respondents	135	54	31	24	26	300
Telephone calls per respondent	7·3	3·9	10·2	4·2	9·3	6·5
Meetings per respondent	2·3	1·4	2·2	1·0	2·0	1·9
Total contacts	9·6	5·3	12·4	5·2	11·3	8·4

Financial	Insurance	Banking	Other finance	All financial
No. of respondents	44	113	67	235
Telephone calls per respondent	5·3	6·2	9·9	7·9
Meetings per respondent	2·7	2·9	1·4	2·5
Total contacts	8·0	9·1	11·3	10·4

Services	Professional	Business	All services	All sectors [a]
No. of respondents	44	49	93	705
Telephone calls per respondent	5·9	9·2	7·8	7·4
Meetings per respondent	1·5	3·3	2·5	2·6
Total contacts	7·4	12·5	10·3	10·0

[a] Includes sectors with less than 20 respondents which are not listed in this table.

TABLE 21. *Intensity of Contact by Status Group*

	Managing director/ chairman/ senior partner	Director/ company secretary/ junior partner	Manager/ section head	Assistant manager/section subhead/ professional	Executive	Total sample
No. of respondents	15	57	365	160	97	705
Telephone	10·2	7·0	7·8	6·5	8·3	7·4
Meeting	3·2	2·3	2·6	1·9	1·3	2·6
All contacts	13·4	9·3	10·4	8·4	9·6	10·0

In addition to status level, differences in contact intensity can be related to the job function of the individual (Tornqvist, 1970). In the absence of a widely accepted classification of office functions, individuals were also classified by the type of office department within which they worked. Type of department is therefore a proxy for job function and, in fact, reveals itself as a more effective discriminator of contact intensity than either business sector or status (Table 22).

Table 22 indicates that individuals in buying departments record the highest average intensity of telephone contacts (17·8) followed by export sales, marketing and shipping and transport and distribution. Public relations and financial departments also have a high intensity of telephone contacts. The lowest level of external telephone contacts are recorded by departments that essentially service the firm, like typing and dispatch and computer services. The highest intensity of meetings are recorded by advertising, buying departments and insurance and finance departments.

THE GEOGRAPHICAL DISTRIBUTION OF CONTACTS

To a large degree high levels of contact activity can be related to the number of contact intensive job functions in the relatively small area of Central London. This is born out by the very high proportion of contacts that are with other firms in Central London. For the full sample, 58% of the telephone contacts and 64% of meetings were with other locations in Central London (Table 23). In spite of differences in cost, there is surprisingly little discrepancy between the two means of communication in terms of the geographical distribution of contacts, again indicating the close connection between the two contact networks. Taking Greater London as a whole, 77% of the telephone calls and 79% of the meetings were internal to the urban area, suggesting a very highly concentrated pattern of contact activity. Whereas proportionately more of the telephone calls were with the rest of the United Kingdom the reverse is the case with meetings; thus 7·7% of the meetings were with firms overseas compared with only 3·0% of the telephone contacts.

There are some striking differences between sectors in the geographical distribution of contacts. The financial sectors have noticeably more contacts confined to Central London (74% of telephone calls and 18% of meetings), when compared to the manufacturing sectors (47% of telephone calls and 53% of meetings).* Manufacturing also has proportionately more overseas meetings (10%). Within the financial group there are some interesting differences between sectors with respect to telephone contacts and meetings; whereas other finance has the most geographically concentrated pattern of telephone contacts, followed by banking and then insurance, the reverse order applies to meetings. The other finance sector does, however, record an above-average proportion of overseas contacts (14%). Within the manufacturing group, paper, printing and publishing records the highest proportion of telephone calls and meetings with other persons in Central London, while construction has a relatively large proportion of overseas meetings (15%). Engineering and chemicals also record an above-average proportion of overseas meetings. The services group falls between manufacturing and finance in terms of geographical concentration of contact, 59% and 71% of telephone contacts and meetings respectively being confined to

*These figures for the financial sectors confirm the results of a study of contact activity in the City of London (Dunning and Morgan, 1971). The City study showed that 52% of all telephone calls and 19% of meetings were with locations in other parts of London.

TABLE 22. *Intensity of Contact by Type of Department*

External relations departments

	Sales	Advertising	Marketing/ market research	Public Relations	Client Relations	Distribution and Buying		Finance departments	
						Export/ transport	Buying	Finance	Insurance
No. of respondents	36	21	52	18	7	18	22	57	26
Calls per respondent	7.8	8.1	6.6	11.3	8.7	13.5	17.8	10.3	6.5
Meetings per respondent	1.6	4.5	2.2	2.7	0.9	1.6	4.5	3.2	3.6
Total contacts	9.4	12.6	8.8	14.0	9.6	13.1	22.3	13.5	10.1

Administrative departments

	Company records/legal/ patents director/ administration	Personnel	Accounts
No. of respondents	117	53	48
Calls per respondent	6.7	5.8	5.8
Meetings per respondent	1.9	2.5	0.7
Total contacts	8.6	8.3	6.5

Internal service departments

	R and D	O and M	Computer services	Typing/ despatch	Professional and technical design	Production
No. of respondents	17	30	20	8	25	50
Calls per respondent	5.5	4.4	2.3	2.5	6.5	7.8
Meetings per respondent	1.4	0.8	1.4	2.6	1.6	2.2
Total contacts	6.9	5.2	3.7	5.1	8.1	10.0

Building services departments

	Property	Architects	Engineers	Surveyors	Maintenance
No. of respondents	13	10	30	12	13
Calls per respondent	10.1	7.0	6.7	7.7	7.3
Meetings per respondent	1.8	1.8	1.8	2.3	3.4
Total contacts	11.9	8.8	8.5	10.0	10.7

	All respondents
	705
	7.4
	2.6
	10.0

TABLE 23. *Geographical Distribution of Contacts by Sector*

Manufacturing	Chemicals	Engineering	Other manu-facturing	Paper, printing publishing	Construction	All manu-facturing
No. of respondents	135	54	31	24	26	300
Telephone contacts:						
Central London (%)	53	50	38	59	41	47
Greater London (%)	18	25	22	19	27	22
South-east region (%)	11	6	9	16	12	11
Rest of United Kingdom (%)	14	13	26	5	18	16
Overseas (%)	4	7	5	1	2	4
Meetings;						
Central London (%)	54	43	57	68	43	53
Greater London (%)	17	33	22	11	12	53
South-east region (%)	8	4	3	10	15	7
Rest of United Kingdom (%)	9	7	10	11	15	10
Overseas (%)	12	12	8	0	15	10

Distribution	All distributions	Finance Insurance	Banking	Other finance	All finance
No. of respondents	22	44	113	67	235
Telephone contacts:					
Central London (%)	40	67	73	80	74
Greater London (%)	21	11	13	11	12
South-east region (%)	21	6	3	3	4
Rest of United Kingdom (%)	16	7	9	4	7
Overseas (%)	2	9	2	2	3
Meetings:					
Central London (%)	60	85	78	63	76
Greater London (%)	17	4	9	16	8
South-east region (%)	4	3	3	1	3
Rest of United	14	2	5	9	6
Kingdom (%)	14	2	5	9	6
Overseas (%)	5	6	5	14	7

Business and Professional services	Professional services	Business services	All business and professional services		All Contacts
No. of respondents	44	49	93		705
Telephone contacts:					
Central London (%)	37	71	59		58
Greater London (%)	20	17	19		19
South-east region (%)	11	4	6		8
Rest of United Kingdom (%)	27	7	14		12
Overseas (%)	5	1	2		3
Meetings:					
Central London (%)	53	83	71		64
Greater London (%)	14	9	11		15
South-east region (%)	6	2	4		5
Rest of United Kingdom (%)	3	5	9		9
Overseas (%)	24	1	5		7

Central London. A marked contrast can be found between professional services and business services. Business services basically serve a local or Central London market, with 71% of all telephone calls and 83% of all meetings being with other persons in Central London. On the other hand, professional services appear to serve a wider market, with 48% of all telephone contacts and 33% of all meetings being with persons working outside Greater London — well in excess of the average figures of 23% of 21% respectively.

TABLE 24. *Travel Time to Meetings and Mode of Travel*

Length of journey	%	Mode of travel	%
Less than 10 minutes	38	Walk	33
10-30 minutes	40	Bus	5
30-60 minutes	10	Private car	21
1-2 hours	7	Taxi	24
More than 2 hours	5	Underground	6
		Train	10
		Plane	1

Number of meetings involving travel = 523

TRAVEL TIME AND MODE OF TRAVEL

The importance of Central London contacts is confirmed by details of travel time and mode of travel to meetings. Approximately two-thirds of the meetings took place outside the respondent's place of work and therefore involved travel (Table 24). One-third of these business trips were on foot and took less than 10 minutes. Altogether, 78% of the business trips took less than 30 minutes. After journeys on foot, taxis and private cars are the most important modes of travel, accounting for 45% of all business trips. Walking to business meetings is most characteristic of the City, the City of London study showing that three-quarters of all business trips generated there take place on foot. In part this is a reflection of the highly organised spatial structure of linked office activities in the City. Elsewhere in the Central Area, space is not so clearly structured and high levels of personal movement (particularly by taxi) are generated (Goddard, 1970b). These figures therefore already begin to suggest a comparable connection between location patterns within the centre and contact patterns.

CHAPTER 6

Inter-sectoral Contact Flows

THE DATA MATRICES

The extent to which the spatial grouping of office activities identified in Part I correspond to sets of functionally related offices can be established by examination of the pattern of inter-sectoral contact flows. From the diaries the question on initiation can be used to give a directional component to communications. With this question acting as a filter, square contact matrices can be constructed in which each column represents a receiving or chosen sector and each row an initiating or choosing sector; diagonal elements contain intra-sector contacts. Separate contact matrices have been constructed for telephone calls and face-to-face meetings with the entries representing the absolute number of contacts recorded between each sector. Each participant in meetings involving more than two people had to be counted as a separate contact, as large meetings could involve people from several different sectors. (Matrices were also constructed with each contact weighted by frequency, but analysis of these matrices produced broadly similar results.) For the purpose of this analysis, 42 office sectors were identified, which represents a considerable aggregation of the three-digit classification. (A full list of these categories is given in Fig. 15 on page 177). The sector groupings were defined in order to obtain a minimum of 25 meetings and 25 telephone contacts originating or terminating in each sector. Clearly the pattern of transactions will depend on the way in which these groupings are defined; too broad a classification will mask critical functional differences between offices, while too fine a classification creates a transaction matrix with an excess of zero entries. The particular classification that has been adopted is therefore entirely pragmatic.

Because of the definitions that have been used in defining inter-sectoral contact flows, sectors not sampled in the survey, like central and local government offices, can appear in the rows and columns of the matrices. This is because individuals in sampled firms could initiate or receive contacts from individuals in sectors outside the study. Obviously no contact will be recorded within or between sectors not represented in the sample. Only 8 out of the 42 sectors that were defined did not contain sampled firms. The problem that these categories create could have been overcome if only sectors with sampled firms had been included in the rows of the matrix, but this would have meant ignoring an important directional component in contact flows.

Because of the very small size of the sample and the considerable variations in sample size between sectors, no attempt has been made to gross up the figures of contact between sectors. An estimate of the total amount of contact between sectors could have been obtained by relating the number of contacts recorded in the survey to the total office employment in each sector on the assumption that contact activity bears a direct and consistent relationship to employment. The preceding chapter has clearly indicated that there are considerable variations between sectors and the number of contacts generated per employee. There also could be significant differences in the composition of the office work force by job function and status between sectors, dimensions which are both related to the gross amount of contact generated. For these reasons the survey data must be considered on its own merits and not necessarily representative of the overall pattern of contacts between office sectors in Central London. In spite of these problems the data do provide a useful basis for a preliminary evaluation of the methods that might be used on a more extensive set of information.

APPROACHES TO THE IDENTIFICATION OF FUNCTIONAL SUBS SUBSYSTEMS

Our first objective is to seek out functional subsystems within the meeting and telephone contact networks defined by the transaction matrices; and, given the supposition that such subsystems do exist, to assign each sector to a group such that within-group linkages are maximized. A variety of numerical procedures suggest themselves. Although most succeed in reducing the complexity of interaction matrices through highlighting incipient group structures, all suffer from the disadvantage that the final decision as to which individual to allocate to each group depends on the specification of usually arbitrary thresholds for group membership. Some element of subjectivity is therefore inevitably involved (Johnston, 1968).

Berry's original work on commodity flows has suggested factor analysis as a technique for identifying functional groups (Berry, 1966). This technique can be applied to the contact matrices by correlating columns and extracting factors that indicate chosen sectors with similar patterns of linkages to sets of choosing sectors. High factor loadings identify the common chosen sectors and high factor scores the choosing sectors. Specifying some arbitrary cut off for the definition of high factor loadings and high factor scores and linking the two sectors together, defines the interacting groups. The analysis can be inverted (*Q*-mode analysis) to provide groupings of choosing sectors in terms of common patterns of choice. Differences in the groupings according to *R*-mode and *Q*-mode analysis are indicative of asymmetric relationships or contacts that are not reciprocated.

Russett has criticised the application of conventional factor analysis to the correlation matrix derived from the transaction data on the grounds that it does not define interacting groups but only individuals with similar patterns of connections (Russett, 1967). Following MacRae and Horst, he suggests direct factor analysis of the original square transaction matrix, with *R*-mode analysis defining the chosen individuals and *Q*-mode analysis the choosing individuals (MacRae, 1960; Horst, 1965). In this study, questions concerning the reliability of the data in an absolute sense unfortunately do not justify the use of direct factor analysis.

While suggesting groupings of sectors, factor analysis has no theoretical underpinning. However, the indifference model of transaction flow analysis, although basically only a simple data transformation, does seem particularly suitable for the prediction of flows that are relatively unconstrained by distance — such as intra-city contacts (Savage and Deutsch, 1960). The transaction flow model requires comparing the actual flows between two sectors with that which would be expected given the chosen sector's share of all contacts. Thus if sector j receives 10% of all incoming contacts, sector i would be expected to direct 10% of its contacts towards sector j. Expected interaction E_{ij} is calculated only when actual contacts occur between respective sectors (Brams, 1966).

$$E_{ij} = O_i \left(\frac{A_{ij}}{\sum\limits_i D_j} \right),$$

where $O_i = \sum\limits_j A_{ij}$, $D_j = \sum\limits_i A_{ij}$, and A_{ij} = actual contacts between i and j,

$$D_{ij} = A_{ij} - E_{ij},$$

$$R_{ij} = \frac{A_{ij} - E_{ij}}{E_{ij}}$$

Absolute or relative differences between observed and expected contacts that exceed specified thresholds can be defined as salient flows. These indicate sectors having strong interconnection relative to the whole system.

Neither factor analysis nor transaction flow analysis will define a complete assignment of sectors to groups. In the case of factor analysis this can be achieved by applying some grouping algorithm to a similarity matrix derived from the factor scores. This approach has been adopted by Goddard in a study of functional regions within the City centre (Goddard, 1970b). However, this will only define groups according to the pattern of choice and not interconnected choosing and chosen sectors. Similarly, a binary matrix indicating salient connections derived from the transaction flow analysis can be subjected to some grouping procedure like dissimilarity analysis (McNaughton-Smith *et al.*, 1964). As this connection matrix is likely to be asymmetrical, the problem of whether to group on the basis of choosing or chosen sectors still arises. In view of these difficulties, conventional factor analysis has been adopted to suggest incipient groups and transaction flow analysis used as a guide in assigning residual sectors to groups.

THE TELEPHONE CONTACT NETWORK

Six factors provide the best description of the telephone contact network. Together, the six factors account for 62% of the total variance. A normal varimax rotation was performed upon an initial principal components solution to give the factor structures described in Table 25.

TABLE 25. *Factor Analysis of Inter-sectoral Telephone Contacts*
(columns as receiving or chosen sectors)

Factor 1: Civil engineering

Chosen sector	FL	Choosing sector	FS
Architects	0·868	General construction	5·103
General construction	0·844	Consulting engineers	1·463
Consulting engineers	0·833	Bricks, pottery, glass and cement	1·309
Specialist construction	0·763		
Metals and metal goods	0·689		
Primary industry	0·673		
Bricks, pottery, glass and cement	0·662		

Explained variance: 12·54%

TABLE 25 (continued)

Factor 2: Fuel and Oil

Chosen sector	FL	Choosing sector	FS
Fuel and oil	−0·904	Fuel and oil	−5·858
Non-profit services	−0·904		
Transport and communications	−0·876		
Mechanical engineering and machinery	−0·797		
Central and local government	−0·648		
Office services	−0·516		

Explained variance: 12·25%

Factor 3: Banking and finance

Chosen sector	FL	Choosing sector	FS
Stockbroking	−0·885	Banking	−3·876
Property	−0·870	Property	−4·300
Banking	−0·862		
Legal services	−0·848		
Other finance	−0·658		
Accounting	−0·524		

Explained variance: 10·95%

Factor 4: Publishing and business services

Chosen sector	FL	Choosing sector	FS
Chemicals and pharmaceuticals	0·881	Chemicals and pharmaceuticals	4·518
Retailing	0·859	Advertising and public relations	2·696
Food, drink and tobacco	0·805	Paper, printing and publishing	2·100
Other special services	0·747		
Paper, printing and publishing	0·716		
Advertising and public relations	0·691		

Explained variance: 10.56%

Factor 5: Official agencies

Chosen sector	FL	Choosing sector	FS
Electrical engineering	−0·906	Entertainment	−5·454
Entertainment	−0·901	Paper, printing and publishing	−1·663
Societies and Associations	−0·711	Miscellaneous business services	−1·191
Miscellaneous business services	−0·675		

Explained variance: 9·05%

Factor 6: Commodity trading

Chosen sector	FL	Choosing sector	FS
Food wholesaling	0·790	Export and import merchants	−4·980
Textiles, leather, and clothing	−0·772	Property	−1·438
Export and import merchants	−0·609	Commodity brokers	−1·426
Transport services	−0·600	Food wholesaling	−1·181
		Retailing	−1·064

Explained variance: 6·70%. Total explained variance: 62·05%

Note: Only factor loadings greater than ± 0·50 and factor scores greater than ± 1·00 are shown.

FL = factor loading. FS = factor scores.

E

Factor one can be described as a civil engineering group, including architects, consulting engineers and brick and cement manufacturers. The group focuses on general construction companies as the principal choosing sector. It is well known that many aspects of a civil engineering project are contracted out to different types of firms; inevitably this procedure will lead to a substantial volume of contact between the various contractors.

Factor 2 centres on fuel and oil companies and is partly a reflection of overrepresentation of this sector in the initial sample. The major links maintained by fuel and oil companies include those with the transport industry, engineering firms and central government. Factor 3 covers the closely related activities of banking and finance; surprisingly, insurance loads only moderately (0·42) on this factor. Factor 4 includes industries very directly concerned with publicity − like advertising agencies, public relations consultants, management consultants, pharmaceutical manufacturers, retailers and food manufacturers. Factor 5 isolates the activities of public and semi-public agencies, including broadcasting (here classified under entertainment), government offices and professional associations. Finally, factor 6 suggests a small group of activities concerned with commodity trading.

On the leading factors, factor scores are generally confined to a few sectors. These sectors are the principal sources of flows for contacts within each group. The high scores also indicate the skewed nature of the underlying distributions; normalizing transformations of the data would partly suppress this basic fact. To some extent, this highly nodal structure reflects the sampling procedure, the choosing sectors tending to be those with a large sample of diaries. This bias is reinforced by the greater likelihood of respondents recording telephone contacts they have initiated, rather than incoming calls. Thus whereas the choosing sectors are predominantly those sampled, the chosen sectors are often those not included in the sample or with small sample fractions. For example, government offices are major choices for contacts in certain groups, but because these offices were not included in the sample, they are not recorded as a major chooser. In fact very few respondents recorded contacts that had been initiated by the government sector.

THE MEETING NETWORK

Six factors also provide the best description of the inter-sectoral meeting contacts, accounting for 52% of the total variance (Table 26).

TABLE 26. *Factor Analysis of Inter-sectoral Meeting Contacts*

Factor 1: Banking and finance

Chosen sector	FL	Choosing sector	FS
Stockbroking	0·908	Banking	5·595
Banking	0·870		
Office services	0·806		
Legal services	0·754		
Other finance	0·658		

Explained variance: 11·21%

Factor 2: Entertainment

Chosen sector	FL	Choosing sector	FS
Entertainment	0·756	Entertainment	5·781
Electrical engineering	0·825		
Non-profit services	0·820		
Other specialist wholesaling	0·805		
Food wholesaling	0·633		

Societies and associations	0·563
Food, drink and tobacco	0·533
Transport and communications	0·513

Explained variance: 10·36%

Factor 3: Fuel and oil

Chosen sector	FL	Choosing sector	FS
Fuel and oil	−0·882	Fuel and oil	−5·609
Mechanical engineering	−0·745		
Other specialist consultancy	−0·692		
Societies and associations	−0·617		
Accountancy	−0·530		

Explained variance: 9·74%

Factor 4: Publishing and business services

Chosen sector	FL	Choosing sector .	FS
Advertising and public relations	−0·847	Paper, printing and publishing	−3·000
Paper, printing and publishing	−0·795	Advertising and public relations	−3·310
Retailing	−0·735	Chemicals	−3·173
Chemicals	−0·651	Precision engineering	−1·005
Miscellaneous business services	−0·527		

Explained variance: 8.91%

Factor 5: Civil engineering

Chosen sector	FL	Choosing sector	FS
Consulting engineers	0·807	General construction	3·076
General construction	0·783	Property	2·651
Architects	0·612	Architects	2·640
Specialist contracting	0·783	Consulting engineers	2·290
		Office services	1·212

Explained variance: 7.40%

Factor 6: Trading

Chosen sector	FL	Choosing sector	FS
Transport equipment	−0·732	Export and import merchants	−4·218
Textiles, leather and clothing	−0·652	Transport equipment	−1·792
Accountancy	−0·639	Other insurance	−1·569
		Precision engineering	−1·263

Explained variance: 5·56%

Total explained variance: 53·18%

The lower level of explanation achieved by the same number of factors suggests that the meeting network is less structured than that maintained by telephone contacts. Three of these factors, namely those associated with civil engineering, publishing and business services and banking and finance can be equated with the similar groupings derived from the analysis of telephone contacts. These three groups, therefore, appear to be the most readily identifiable contact subsystems. As the leading factor, the banking and finance group is the most interconnected according to meeting contacts, whereas it ranks third according to telephone contacts. From this it might be inferred that this group makes greater use of the meeting for communication relative to all other groups. This and other differences between telephone and meetings suggest that each communication channel is used for somewhat different contact networks.

However, in view of the nature of the data, inferences about the nature of meeting contacts need to be considered cautiously. Meetings take place with a much lower frequency than telephone contacts. For the full sample, 41% of the telephone contacts took place more than once a week compared with only 24% of the meetings; if the financial sectors, with a high frequency of meetings are excluded, the latter figure is substantially reduced. The 3 days of the diary survey therefore represent a much smaller sample of meetings than of telephone contacts. In addition, the problem of dealing with meetings involving two respondents and the convention of treating each participant as a separate contact may bias the meeting network towards sectors with a high proportion of large meetings. For these reasons, the analysis of telephone contacts can be taken as more representative of the basic pattern of functional groupings.

FUNCTIONAL COMPLEXES AND SPATIAL CLUSTERS

In spite of the small sample size, office complexes isolated in this study of contact flows show a high degree of correspondence with the spatial clusters identified in Chapter 3. Although ordered differently in terms of explained variance, all but the fuel and public agency factors derived from the functional analysis of telephone contacts appear to have approximate spatial equivalents. The activities associated with banking and finance, commodity trading, civil engineering and publishing, together with certain business services like advertising, therefore appear to have been tied to these groups by a form of functional relationship that also requires close spatial proximity. How far this is true can only be established by an analysis of the characteristics of the linkages between the different sectors. A large amount of routine communication might be carried on between two sectors in an office complex by extensive networks of face-to-face meetings simply because the related firms are located close to one another. An examination of the nature of these communications might indicate that the contacts could be carried out at lower cost at a greater distance using telecommunications.

Referring back to the spatial analysis also reveals that when clusters are identified on the ground, a considerable degree of overlap is apparent between different areas of economic specialisation. In functional terms, therefore, one would also expect a commensurate degree of contact between the various office complexes. This question is taken up in the next section.

THE PATTERN OF WITHIN- AND BETWEEN-GROUP LINKAGES

From the results of the factor analyses of contact patterns it cannot be assumed that all chosen sectors loading high on a particular factor are both significantly connected with each other or with each of the principal choosing sectors indicated by the high factor scores. In previous studies of functional regions, this assumption has been made, and all high loadings and high scoring places linked together in mapping the regionalisation. This exact pattern of linkage is best examined through transaction flow analysis.

In developing the final grouping that is displayed in Fig. 15 the highly connected sectors according to telephone contacts have been formed into clusters as suggested by the factor analysis, with the final assignment of residual sectors being made according to the pattern of salient transactions. In this procedure, greater weight has been given to two-way linkages. Heavy lines in the diagram indicate linkages where either or both R_{ij} and R_{ji} exceed 0·50 and D_{ij} and D_{ji} exceed 2·0. Lighter lines indicate linkages where there is a one-way connection exceeding the same threshold for both R_{ij} and D_{ij}. These particular thresholds indicate pairs of sectors that have 50% more interaction than expected (relative saliency) and where this involves more than two actual contacts (absolute saliency).

The diagram highlights a substantial number of between-group linkages and so illustrates a basic conceptual limitation of factor analysis when applied to transaction data. This is that the factor analysis model seeks to reduce the data into the minimum number of statistically independent groups, whereas complex interaction systems are composed of interdependent or overlapping systems.* (Johnston, 1970). Oblique factor rotation solutions can only marginally improve on this basic orthogonality imposed by the initial factoring procedure. In this instance, promax rotation of the varimax factor loadings only suggested a slight degree of correlation between factors in spite of the strong evidence to the contrary (Hendrickson and White, 1964).

The pattern of within- and between-group linkages are summarised in Table 27 and Figs. 15–18. According to both the absolute volume of contact and the number of two-way salient transactions, within-group linkages exceed the number of linkages to any other single group. Overall, 54·2% of telephone contacts are within the groups. The most strongly internalised group is that composed of the financial sectors, with 71·2% of contacts originating in the group being destined for other sectors in the same group. In contrast, another major group, civil engineering, has only 43·1% of its telephone contacts internal to the group, with substantial volumes of communication to the financial group and the publishing and business services group. Examination of Fig. 15 suggests that the former connections can be attributed to links between property companies and architects and the latter to links between consulting engineers and chemical manufacturers. The trading group also has a large number of external links, particularly to trading and finance, while the public agencies group has strong links with publishing and business services.

Within- and between-group meeting contacts are summarised in Figs. 17 and 18. In Fig. 17 the sectors are clustered into groups defined from the analysis of telephone contacts. The pattern of salient transactions at once confirms the different nature of the meeting network and the overall lower degree of connectivity at the same saliency level. Some sectors are completely unconnected with the number of between-group links often exceeding the number of within-group links. However, when the absolute volume of contacts within and between groups are considered, the proportion of meetings that are confined to the group (60%) exceeds the equivalent figure for telephone contacts (54%) (Table 27). We can therefore conclude that the meeting network is the less interconnected simply because contacts are more tightly confined to a few sectors. This fact can be confirmed by examining how far the proportion of contacts received by a chosen sector j from every other sector i deviates from each of the choosing sector i's share of all contacts. An index of concentration may be defined as

$$C_j = \sum_{i=1}^{N} (A_{ij}/D_j) - (O_i / \sum_{i-1}^{N} O_i),$$

Σ for all positive differences,

$$O_i = \sum_{j=1}^{N} A_{ij} \quad D_j = \sum_{j=1}^{N} A_{ij}.$$

*The small differences in the amount of variance associated with each successive rotated component is also indicative of high degree of overlap between the clusters – which could lead to instability in the rotation procedure.

The mean value of C for meetings for all sectors j is 0·693 compared with a mean of 0·553 for telephone contacts. About this mean there is a considerable variation between sectors in the degree of concentration of their contact flows.

TABLE 27. *Within- and Between-group Contacts*
(A) Telephone calls

From	To						Total	%
	A	B	C	D	E	F		
A	317·0	121·0	23·0	127·0	50·0	97·0	735·0	14·5
%	43·1	16·4	3·1	17·3	6·8	13·1		
B	83·0	1000·0	45·0	116·0	53·0	107·0	1404·0	27·7
%	5·9	71·2	3·2	8·3	3·8	7·6		
C	34·0	50·0	111·0	35·0	11·0	26·0	267·0	5·3
%	12·7	18·7	41·6	13·1	4·1	9·7		
D	115·0	177·0	38·0	646·0	109·0	137·0	1222·0	24·1
%	9·4	14·5	3·1	52·8	8·9	11·2		
E	61·0	65·0	11·0	85·0	207·0	94·0	523·0	10·3
%	11·6	12·4	2·1	16·2	39·5	18·0		
F	97·0	109·0	28·0	126·0	85·0	462·0	907·0	17·9
%	10·7	12·0	3·1	13·2	9·4	50·9		
Total	707·0	1522·0	256·0	1135·0	515·0	923·0	5058·0	
%	13·9	30·0	5·1	22·4	10·1	18·2		

(B) Meetings

	A	B	C	D	E	F	Total	%
A	209·0	35·0	0·0	41·0	44·0	47·0	376·0	15·2
%	55·5	9·3	0·0	9·6	11·6	12·3		
B	50·0	472·0	9·0	60·0	15·0	21·0	627·0	25·0
%	8·0	75·0	1·4	9·6	1·6	3·3		
C	3·0	8·0	27·0	8·0	15·0	15·0	76	3·1
%	3·9	10·5	35·5	10·5	17·7	19·7		
D	52·0	90·0	8·0	348·0	48·0	54·0	600·0	24·3
%	8·6	15·0	1·3	58·0	8·0	9·0		
E	26·0	34·0	13·0	35·0	95·0	48·0	251·1	10·1
%	10·3	13·5	5·2	13·9	37·3	19·1		
F	50·0	44·0	6·0	68·0	44·0	329·0	541·0	21·9
%	9·2	8·1	1·1	12·6	8·1	60·8		
Total	390·0	683·0	63·0	560·0	261·0	541·0	2471·0	
%	13·7	27·6	2·5	22·6	10·5	21·9		

A, Civil engineering. B, Banking and finance. C, Commodity trading.
D, Publishing and business services. E, Public agencies. F, Fuel and oil.

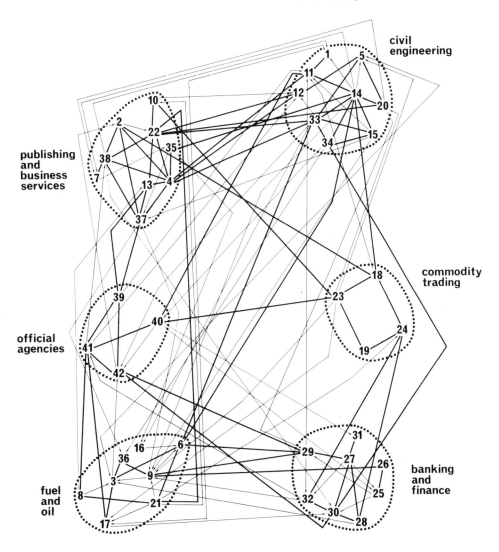

Fig. 15. Telephone contacts: salient transactions.

Key to Fig. 15. 1, Primary industry. 2, Food, drink and tobacco. 3, Fuel and oil. 4, Chemicals.
5, Metals and metal goods. 6, Mechanical engineering and machinery. 7, Precision engineering.
8, Electrical engineering. 9, Transport equipment. 10, Textiles, leather and clothing.
11, Bricks, pottery, glass and cement. 12, Other manufacturing. 13, Paper, printing and publishing.
14, General construction. 15, Specialist contracting. 16, Gas, electricity and water. 17, Transport
and communications. 18, Transport services. 19, Food wholesaling. 20, Other specialist
wholesaling. 21, General wholesale merchants. 22, Retailing. 23, Export and import merchants.
24, Commodity brokers. 25, Insurance companies. 26, Other insurance. 27, Banking.
28, Stockbroking and jobbing. 29, Other finance. 30, Property. 31, Accounting. 32, Legal
services. 33, Consulting engineers. 34, Architects. 35, Other specialist consultancy. 36, Non-profit
services. 37, Advertising and public relations.

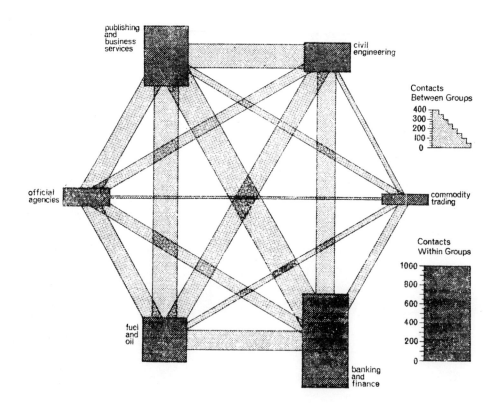

Fig. 16. Telephone contacts: between groups flows.

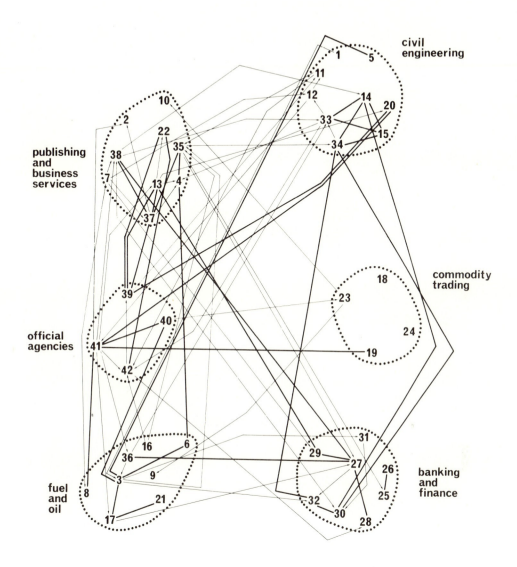

Fig. 17. Meetings: salient transactions

Key to Fig. 17. 1, Primary industry. 2, Food, drink and tobacco. 3, Fuel and oil, 4, Chemicals.
5, Metals and metal goods. 6, Mechanical engineering and machinery. 7, Precision engineering.
8, Electrical engineering. 9, Transport equipment. 10, Textiles, leather and clothing.
11, Bricks, pottery, glass and cement. 12, Other manufacturing. 13, Paper, printing and publishing.
14, General construction. 15, Specialist contracting. 16, Gas, electricity and water. 17, Transport
and communications. 18, Transport services. 19. Food wholesaling. 20, Other specialist
wholesaling. 21, General wholesale merchants. 22, Retailing. 23, Export and import merchants.
24, Commodity brokers. 25, Insurance companies. 26, Other insurance. 27, Banking.
28, Stockbroking and jobbing. 29, Other finance. 30, Property. 31, Accounting. 32, Legal
services. 33, Consulting engineers. 34, Architects. 35, Other specialist consultancy. 36, Non-profit
services. 37, Advertising and public relations.

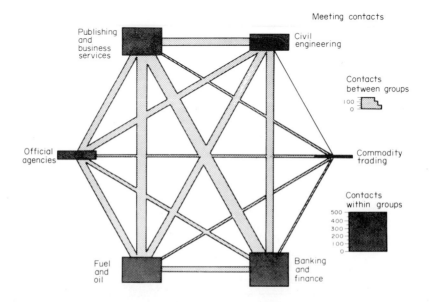

Fig. 18. Meetings: between group flows.

THE CONNECTIVITY OF BUSINESS SECTORS TO THE CONTACT NETWORK

A number of distinctive functional groupings of office sectors have been identified and the volume of within- and between- groups contacts specified. In terms of locational policy, some summary measures that suggest the degree of involvement of each sector in the functional groups is required. One such index is provided by the final communality for each sector derived from the factor analyses of the contact data. The sectors with high communalities will be those with high factor loadings and hence a heavy involvement in one or more groups.

Some sectors may not be involved in any particular functional group and therefore have a low communality, yet still be well connected to the contact network, especially through indirect links. Factor analysis can be criticised on the grounds that it considers only direct linkages in the system. Where flows are unconstrained, as is the case of intersectoral contacts, linkages are most likely to be direct. However, in certain instances, indirect linkages from intermediate sectors may be significant. For example, a firm wishing to place an advertisement usually approaches the medium, such as a newspaper publisher, through an advertising agency. There is only, therefore, an indirect link between the firm and the newspaper publisher. To take account of this situation, an index of connectivity can be derived from the powering of the connection matrix that has been defined from the transaction flow analysis. The two-way salient transaction displayed in Fig. 14 defines a symmetrical graph (C^1) with a diameter of 6: from the sum of the power series $C^1 + C^2 + C^3 \cdots \cdots C^6$, a new matrix of total connectivity can be determined. Summing the columns of the matrix gives a measure of connectivity for each sector that considers both direct and indirect links. This analysis cannot be carried out for the meeting network since at the same saliency level a completely connected graph cannot be defined.

The converse of a high degree of connectivity is that a particular sector has a large proportion of its contacts with a limited number of other sectors. Because the connectivity measure is based on a crude binary generalisation of this contact network, a supplementary measure is provided by the index of concentration outlined earlier. The sectors with a low concentration index will be those connected directly to a large number of other businesses.

All three indices are relevant measures of the attachment of each business sector to the Central London contact system. These measures are summarised in Table 28. Each index has been ranked and divided into quartiles and the sectors divided into three groups on the basis of their combined ranking. At the extreme of the ranking, the various measures are broadly similar. Sectors like primary industry, textiles, commodity broking and insurance fall into the bottom halves of the distributions according to all five indices, i.e. these sectors have highly concentrated contact flows, few indirect linkages and have little involvement in any of the groups. Sectors like general construction, retailing, banking and central government fall into the top halves of all of the distributions, with dispersed contacts, numerous indirect connections and high group involvement. In the intermediate group some sectors, like specialist construction, have numerous indirect connections, yet with a relatively weak involvement in any group and a concentrated pattern of contact flows. Some sectors, notably banking, other finance and advertising, rank higher according to meetings than telephone contacts.

TABLE 28. *Connectivity of Business Sectors to the Contact Network*

Sector	Telephone Contacts			Meetings	
	Concentration index	Communality	Connectivity index (C^6)	Concentration index	Communality
Highly connected					
Fuel and oil	0·45 (1)	0·85 (1)	306 (2)	0·56 (1)	0·78 (1)
Metals and metal goods	0·55 (2)	0·73 (2)	344 (1)	0·64 (2)	0·53 (3)
Mechanical engineering and machinery	0·52 (2)	0·90 (1)	365 (1)	0·67 (2)	0·64 (2)
Paper, printing and publishing	0·43 (1)	0·72 (3)	298 (2)	0·44 (1)	0·79 (1)
General construction	0·40 (1)	0·85 (1)	622 (1)	0·63 (2)	0·64 (2)
Retailing	0·46 (1)	0·76 (2)	319 (1)	0·76 (3)	0·61 (2)
Banking	0·46 (1)	0·75 (2)	160 (3)	0·52 (1)	0·78 (1)
Legal services	0·44 (1)	0·85 (1)	140 (3)	0·60 (2)	0·83 (1)
Consulting engineers	0·51 (2)	0·73 (2)	546 (2)	0·59 (1)	0·75 (2)
Other specialist consultancy	0·48 (2)	0·67 (3)	288 (2)	0·49 (1)	0·81 (1)
Advertising and public relations	0·57 (3)	0·57 (3)	271 (2)	0·50 (1)	0·83 (1)
Office services	0·34 (1)	0·74 (2)	119 (3)	0·55 (1)	0·81 (1)
Societies and associations	0·40 (1)	0·74 (2)	195 (2)	0·63 (2)	0·80 (1)
Central and local government	0·39 (1)	0·86 (1)	160 (3)	0·52 (1)	0·60 (3)
Moderately connected					
Food, drink and tobacco	0·65 (4)	0·69 (3)	206 (2)	0·61 (2)	0·62 (2)
Chemicals	0·57 (3)	0·81 (2)	507 (1)	0·64 (2)	0·59 (3)
Precision engineering	0·47 (2)	0·12 (4)	139 (3)	0·70 (2)	0·17 (4)
Electrical engineering	0·60 (3)	0·84 (1)	51 (4)	0·69 (3)	0·78 (1)
Bricks, pottery, glass and cement	0·57 (3)	0·54 (3)	405 (1)	0·75 (3)	0·16 (4)
Other manufacturing	0·55 (3)	0·31 (4)	417 (1)	0·57 (1)	0·29 (4)
Specialist contracting	0·57 (3)	0·71 (3)	410 (1)	0·79 (4)	0·40 (3)
Transport and communications	0·61 (3)	0·90 (1)	119 (4)	0·79 (4)	0·52 (3)
Transport services	0·60 (3)	0·72 (2)	203 (2)	0·81 (4)	0·09 (4)
Other specialist wholesaling	0·43 (1)	0·57 (3)	306 (2)	0·79 (4)	0·71 (2)
Stockbroking and jobbing	0·64 (4)	0·85 (1)	47 (4)	0·75 (4)	0·84 (4)
Other finance	0·54 (1)	0·48 (1)	222 (4)	0·56 (4)	0·75 (2)
Architects	0·54 (2)	0·82 (2)	345 (1)	0·81 (4)	0·39 (4)

Sector	Telephone contacts			Meetings	
	Concentration index	Communality	Connectivity index (C^6)	Concentration index	Communality
Moderately connected					
Non-profit services	0·49 (2)	0·91 (1)	59 (4)	0·82 (4)	0·78 (2)
Miscellaneous business services	0·55 (2)	0·62 (3)	165 (3)	0·77 (3)	0·35 (4)
Entertainment	0·57 (3)	0·83 (2)	129 (3)	0·61 (2)	0·76 (2)
Weekly connected					
Primary industry	0·75 (4)	0·51 (4)	73 (4)	0·78 (3)	0·40 (3)
Transport equipment	0·63 (4)	0·22 (4)	226 (2)	0·74 (3)	0·59 (3)
Textiles, leather and clothing	0·70 (4)	0·61 (3)	92 (4)	0·98 (4)	0·45 (3)
Gas, electricity and water	0·67 (4)	0·21 (4)	125 (3)	0·70 (3)	0·05 (4)
Food wholesaling	0·74 (4)	0·66 (3)	50 (4)	0·80 (3)	0·51 (3)
General wholesale merchants	0·76 (4)	0·04 (4)	135 (3)	0·86 (4)	0·09 (4)
Export and import merchants	0·63 (4)	0·48 (4)	162 (3)	0·76 (3)	0·09 (4)
Commodity brokers	0·49 (4)	0·16 (4)	82 (4)	0·84 (4)	0·36 (4)
Insurance companies	0·55 (3)	0·19 (4)	8 (4)	0·78 (4)	0·10 (4)
Other insurance	0·62 (4)	0·09 (4)	43 (4)	0·82 (4)	0·05 (4)
Accounting	0·53 (2)	0·54 (4)	56 (4)	0·79 (4)	0·72 (2)

Numbers in brackets refer to quartile of each sector according to ranking of each index.

These indices are only suggestive of the sort of measures that might provide guidelines in forming a location policy for office sectors. With such a relatively small sample of contacts and the variations of response, too much significance cannot be attached to the specific results. The data were not collected with the sole purpose of measuring the volume of inter-sectoral contact flows. Rather, the primary objective was to establish how far particular information linkages demanded the close spatial proximity of the activities concerned. By examining the characteristics of the communications, it may be possible to identify information links that might be carried out by present or future forms of telecommunications over a considerable distance. By breaking down the crude volume of contacts, some weighting of these linkages might be possible.

CHAPTER 7

The Characteristics of Business Contacts

INTRODUCTION

In addition to questions relating to the sectoral and geographical distributions of contacts and mode of travel, the diary was used to record a number of basic characteristics of business contacts that were possibly relevant to the choice of communications media. These characteristics were suggested by a review of the literature on interpersonal communications (Goddard, 1971). The questions were designed to be generally applicable to all types of organisations. As far as possible they avoid purely subjective ratings of contacts using semantic scales to identify nebulous concepts like 'importance' and 'urgency'. Rather the questions relate to more readily quantifiable characteristics each measuring a different facet of the contact. Taken together these make possible a multivariate classification of contacts that might be indicative of the overall strength of a particular communication link.

Length can be shown to be an important dimension since long contacts are difficult to maintain with telecommunications. Arrangement could be used *in conjunction with* other characteristics as a proxy for concepts like 'urgency' and 'importance'. Urgent matters tend to crop up quickly and lead to unarranged contacts; in this situation the telephone has an advantage, especially over long distances. On the other hand, many routine contacts are unarranged because of the trivial nature of the transactions involved. At the other end of the scale, important subject-matters are often discussed at meetings that have to be arranged a long time in advance *because* a number of busy people are likely to be involved. In the case of meetings, the number of people that need to be involved in a contact is also a vital factor when considering the possibility of using telecommunications, although developments like confra-vision and conference phone calls are likely to change this situation. The frequency with which contacts take place between particular individuals or groups of individuals can be related to their 'familiarity'. Familiar people generally find it easier to assess the other person's reaction on the telephone. Giving or receiving of orders, information and advice are uni-directional communications, while exchanging information, bargaining and general discussion, implies some interplay between the participants. Again, face-to-face contacts have been shown to be more effective for communications involving a substantial amount of feedback. The range of subject-matter discussed is also an important variable since wide-ranging discussions are generally more difficult to maintain on the telephone. Finally, the question of sales and purchases on the contact record sheet was introduced on the assumption that, while ultimately all contacts are concerned with the sales of a firm's goods or services, some are more directly related to the day-to-day process of selling, while others are more concerned with the longer-term search for new markets and products. This question therefore relates to the position of the contact on the time continuum with respect to selling.

FACE-TO-FACE MEETINGS AND TELEPHONE CONTACTS

The contact patterns for the full sample of 1544 meetings and 5266 telephone calls are recorded in Table 29. The responses to each question are presented in percentages to facilitate comparisons between telephone and personal contacts. The most noticeable feature of the telephone contacts is that the bulk are very short, unarranged and concerned with specific subjects. Meetings fall into all of the time categories, although the largest proportion are fairly short (10—30 minutes). The bulk of these meetings (58%) are arranged at least 2 days in advance. Sixty-three per cent of the meetings were between persons meeting only occasionally or for the first time; telephone calls were generally between more familiar participants, with 51% of the respondents contacting each other on at least a weekly basis, while only 24% of the meetings took place once a week or more frequently. Forty-three per cent of the meetings were concerned with at least several subjects compared with only 16% of the telephone contacts. In terms of purpose, telephone contacts were most frequently used for giving orders and giving and receiving information (51% of the total), and meetings most frequently for bargaining, exchanging information and general discussion (55% of the total) — in other words, contacts involving two-way interaction or feedback; only 21% of the telephone contacts fell into categories implying a need for feedback. There is little difference between telephone contacts and meetings in terms of concern with sales or purchases. Considering the characteristics of meetings alone, the bulk of these took place between a limited number of people — 61% were two person meetings and 87% involved five people or less.

INTERRELATIONSHIPS BETWEEN CONTACT CHARACTERISTICS

There are some differences in the characteristics of contacts between business sectors, different types of departments and different status groups. For instance, high status groups have proportionately more long contacts arranged a long time in advance and taking place infrequently, while the reverse is the case in lower status groups. Financial sectors have proportionately more short and frequent contacts between two persons than do manufacturing sectors. But, more striking than the differences between groups, is the consistent relationship between each of the features of a contact within a group. For example, a high proportion of frequent contacts is very likely associated with a high proportion of short contacts involving a limited number of people in specific discussions.

Such correlations between the different features of business contacts can be examined for the full sample by cross-tabulating the reponses to each of the diary questions against one another. There is little point in carrying out this analysis for telephone contacts since these reveal a high degree of consistency for all groupings of the data, which seems to suggest that the telephone is always used for a particular type of low-level communication task. Unlike the telephone, the meeting is a much more flexible medium and can be used for a variety of types of communication from very simple information exchange to complex problem-solving discussions.

TABLE 29. *The Characteristics of Telephone and Meeting Contacts for the Whole Sample*

	Telephone (%)	F/F (%)
Length of Contact		
2-10 minutes	87	19
10-30 minutes	12	29
30-60 minutes	1	19
1-2 hours	0	18
More than 2 hours	0	15
Arrangement of contact		
Not arranged	83	17
Same day	9	13
Day before	4	12
2-7 days	2	31
More than week	2	27
Initiation of contact		
Myself/another person in firm	52	49
Person outside firm	48	51
Frequency of contact		
Daily	18	14
Once a week	23	10
Once a month	14	13
Occasional	34	38
First contact	11	25
Range of subject matter		
One specific subject	84	57
Several specific subjects	15	35
Wide range of subjects	1	8
Concerned with sales or purchases		
Directly	36	38
Indirectly	23	25
Not at all	41	37
Main purpose of contact		
Give order or instruction	13	7
Receive order or instruction	3	1
Give advice	5	6
Receive advice	9	5
Bargaining	3	8
Give information	11	7
Receive information	26	9
Exchange information	20	28
General discussion	7	13
Other	5	16
Total number of contacts	5266	1554
For meetings only		
Number of people at meeting		
One other		61
2-4 people		26
5-10 people		8
More than 10 people		5
For meetings outside workplace	Total	523

F

TABLE 29 (Continued)

	Telephone (%)	F/F (%)
Principal methods of transport		
Walk		33
Bus		5
Private car		21
Taxi		24
Underground		6
Train		10
Plane		1
Length of journey		
Less than 10 minutes		38
10-30 minutes		40
30-60 minutes		10
1-2 hours		7
More than 2 hours		5

CORRELATES OF FREQENCY OF CONTACT

Frequency of contact is an important variable since it is a guide to the familiarity of the participants and an important factor in the choice of communication medium. It is also an indication of the strength of functional linkages. First, there is a highly significant association between the frequency with which meetings take place and their length. In general, individuals in frequent contact are most likely to have short meetings. In fact, 70% of the meetings that take place on a daily basis last less than 10 minutes. However, there is less likelihood of an occasional meeting necessarily lasting a long time — only 18% of the occasional meetings and 15% of the new contacts lasted more than 2 hours. Nevertheless, looking at this relationship the other way round, 45% of the meetings lasting over 2 hours and 49% of those lasting 1-2 hours were occasional contacts, while 51% of the meetings lasting less than 10 minutes took place on a daily basis.

Not surprisingly, daily meetings are usually between two persons — 90% of the contacts falling into this category. New contacts are most likely to occur in meetings involving five or more people. This relationship gives an overall positive association between frequency of contact and size of meeting (chi square = 128·9; significant at 0·1% level). Similarly, there is a connection between the frequency of a meeting and its purpose. Sixty-seven per cent of the meetings concerned with general discussion were first or occasional contacts, while 51% of the contacts concerned with giving or receiving orders took place on a daily basis or at least once a week. In contrast, advice was more likely to be given at meetings involving people in contact on only an occasional basis while bargaining is more likely to take place between people in daily contact. Taking all the categories together, there is a highly significant association between the frequency with which a contact takes place and its purpose (chi square = 400·0 significant at 0·1% level). Frequency is also related to the purpose of telephone contacts. For instance, 25·5% of the telephone contacts taking place on a daily basis were concerned with giving orders compared with 5·7% of the new telephone contacts. Overall, there is a highly significant association between frequency of telephone contacts and the purpose of the call. (chi square = 379·5 significant at the 0·1% level). While there is little relationship between frequency of meetings and range of subject-matter there is a highly significant inverse relationship between frequency of telephone contact and range of subject-matter discussed, i.e., the less frequent the contact the more specific the discussion. The relationship between frequency of meeting and concern with sales and purchases is also distinctive, with 84% of the daily meetings being concerned directly with sales and purchases and 54% of the first contacts being unconcerned with buying or selling. In other words, the less familiar the participants, the more likely that the meeting would be unrelated to purchasing. A less-strong relationship applied to telephone contacts.

PREARRANGEMENT OF MEETINGS

Prearrangement of the meeting can be used as a guide to the urgency or importance of the subject-matter and the suitability of telecommunications as a medium for the contact. Urgent matters tend to crop up at short notice and are likely to lead to unarranged contacts: however, such contacts may also be of a trivial nature. In either instance, such unarranged contacts could possibly be carried out by telephone. In contrast, important subjects are usually considered by senior personnel who have busy schedules and hence need to arrange meetings a long time in advance. Exception to this connection between importance and prearrangement is often found in the routine meetings prearranged for a fixed time interval (e.g. every month).

Because prearranged meetings generally tend to be concerned with important or difficult subjects that need extensive discussion, these meetings tend to last a long time. Of all meetings lasting more than 2 hours, 51·7% had been arranged more than a week in advance. At the other extreme, unarranged meetings are usually concerned with simple matters that can be dealt with quickly; consequently, 44·9% of the unarranged meetings lasted less than 10 minutes and 89·5% less than 30 minutes. Nevertheless, a significant proportion of the short meetings (29·1%) had been arranged a long time in advance. In spite of this, there is a strong association between the extent of prearrangement and the length of meeting (chi square = 442·6, significant at the 0·1% level). Another reason for meetings being arranged a long time in advance is that a large number of people are involved. There is, therefore, a strong association between the size of the meetings and prearrangement (chi square = 301·0, significant at the 0·1% level). Some 90·8% of the meetings with more than ten people involved have therefore been arranged more than a week in advance and 48·0% of these meetings are meetings with 5-10 people. Conversely, 90·2% of the unarranged meetings involved only two people.

Generally, the longer the meeting was arranged in advance the more likely that its purpose would be general discussion, exchange of information or bargaining, i.e., two-way interaction as opposed to simple giving of orders or information, the latter being more characteristic of unarranged contacts or contacts arranged a short time in advance. The overall relationship between arrangement and purpose is highly significant (chi square = 247·5, significant at 0·1% level). Following from this, there is a corresponding association between prearrangement and subject-matter discussed (chi square = 35·5, significant at 0·1% level), with 46·5% of the meetings concerned with a wide range of subjects, being arranged more than a week in advance, whereas 57·5% of the unarranged meetings were concerned with one specific subject. The bulk of these unarranged meetings (51·1%) were also directly concerned with sales or purchases, whereas 65·5% of the meetings unrelated to sales or purchases were arranged at least a week in advance. The overall relationship between arrangement and sales and purchases is therefore highly significant (chi square = 52·6, significant at the 0·1% level).

LENGTH OF MEETINGS

A strong positive association has been established between length of meeting, the frequency with which the individuals are in contact and how far in advance the meeting has been arranged. Length of meeting can be used as yet another guide to the importance of the subject-matter under discussion. In general, the longer the meeting the more likely it is that its purpose will be information exchange or general discussion: 57·6% of meetings lasting more than one hour fell into this category compared with 19·8% of meetings lasting less than 10 minutes.

In contrast, meetings concerned with giving or receiving orders are most likely to be short: in fact 74·4% of all such meetings last less than half an hour. Meetings concerned with bargaining are also predominantly short, 50·3% lasting less than 10 minutes. This gives an overall highly significant association between length and purpose of meeting (chi square = 268·5, significant at the 0·1% level). Not surprisingly, short meetings are usually concerned with one specific subject (81·3% of all meetings lasting less than 10 minutes are concerned with one specific subject), whereas longer meetings are more likely to be concerned with a wide range of general subjects (58·2% of the meetings classified in this way lasted over an hour). The overall association between length of meeting and the range of subject-matter discussed is therefore very strong (chi-square = 138·9, significant at the 0·1% level). Finally, long meetings are less likely to be concerned with sales or purchases than short meetings: 48·2% of the meetings lasting more than 2 hours were not concerned with sales or purchases, whereas 64·6% of those lasting less than 10 minutes were directly concerned with buying or selling. The association between length of meeting and concern with sales or purchases is therefore highly significant (chi square = 132·8, significant at the 0·1% level).

SIZE OF MEETINGS

It has been demonstrated that the number of people involved in a meeting is significantly associated with the frequency with which the participants have contact, how long the meeting was arranged in advance and the length of that meeting. The most pronounced correlate of size of meeting is its length: 93·4% of the meetings lasting less than 10 minutes involved only two persons, whereas 85·6% of the meetings involving more than five people lasted over 2 hours. The overall association is very high (chi square = 546·8, significant at the 0·1% level). In general, the more people involved in the meeting, the more likely that its purpose is one of general discussion: 32·9% of meetings involving more than ten persons were classified in this way, compared with 17·4% of the two-person meetings. At the other extreme, 97·5% of the meetings involving the giving or receiving of orders or advice were two-person meetings. The overall relationship between size of meetings and purpose is highly significant (chi square = 91·4, significant at the 0·1% level). Following from this association, there is a significant connection between size of meeting and location.

LOCATION OF CONTACT

Many of the characteristics of contact are related to the location of the other firm. In terms of frequency, 94·4% of the daily meetings are with other firms located in Central London compared with 62·7% of the first contacts and 70·1% of all daily contacts. Similarly, 78·8% of daily telephone contacts are most likely to be with Central London firms compared with only 42·7% of the new contacts and 51·6% of the occasional contacts.

Unarranged meetings are more likely to be with firms in Central London than meetings arranged a long time in advance (83·3% of the unarranged meetings are with Central London firms compared with 69·6% of meetings arranged more than a week in advance). Length of meeting is also related to location with 78·8% of meetings lasting less than 30 minutes being with other firms in Central London compared with 56·2% of meetings lasting over 2 hours.

MEETINGS INVOLVING TRAVEL

The characteristics of the 508 meetings involving travel can now be examined. First, there is an obvious close connection between the mode of travel and the length of business trip: 76·1% of the journeys lasting less than 10 minutes took place on foot and 14·7% by taxi; 50% of the journeys lasting over 2 hours were made by train and 46·4% by private car. Cars are also important for an intermediate length journey — 57·4% of those lasting 30-60 minutes used this mode of transport. The Underground was most important for journeys lasting 10–30 minutes, accounting for 43·4% of the total number of business trips falling into this category: 89·3% of the bus journeys were also 10–30 minutes. The overall relationship between length of journey and mode of transport is therefore highly significant at the 0·1% level.

These meetings involving travel also have a number of other interesting distinguishing characteristics. Daily contacts are most likely to involve journeys on foot or by taxi — both lasting less than 10 minutes; in other words, journeys to places very near to the respondent's place of work. Specifically, 60·4% of the meetings taking place on a daily basis involve journeys on foot and 95% of the journeys to daily meetings involve less than 10 minutes' travelling: 21·1% of the daily meetings involve taxi trips. The converse of this relationship is that trips requiring journeys of over an hour are likely to take place on an occasional basis or to be first contacts, with the car or train as the most likely mode of travel. Unarranged meetings are most likely to involve short journeys on foot: 74·3% of the unarranged meetings involving travel were made by foot and 65·7% of the meetings in this category required journeys of less than 10 minutes and 88·6% journeys of under 30 minutes. After walking (49·3% of all trips), taxis are the most important mode of travel for contacts taking place on a weekly basis (30·7% of all trips). Not surprisingly, rail journeys are most likely to be associated with meetings arranged well in advance; there is therefore a highly significant association between prearrangement of contact, mode of travel and length of journey. There is also a significant association between mode of travel, length of journey and length of meeting: 41·7% of the meetings lasting less than 10 minutes were reached on foot as were 53·0% of the meetings in the 10-30 minute category. Some 87·6% of these journeys to meetings lasting less than 30 minutes also took less than 30 minutes' travelling time. The bulk of the meetings lasting over 2 hours involved journeys by car or taxi (31·5% and 27·3% of the total respectively) and 67·9% of the journeys lasting over 2 hours were also followed by meetings lasting over 2 hours.

CHAPTER 8

A Classification of Business Contacts

A MODEL OF CONTACT ACTIVITY

The systematic patterns of co-variation that emerge from cross-tabulating the characteristics of meetings against one another suggest that some fundamental communication process underlies these revealed patterns. A possible model of organisational — environmental relations has been suggested by Thorngren as a basis for understanding contact patterns (Fig. 19). Basic to this model is the notion that all organisational processes and related contacts can be related to some specific sections of a continuous time horizon. Perhaps the most significant information flow in a qualitative sense are those connected with long-term scanning of socio-economic environments in order to identify future possibilities and alternatives. Thorngren argues that in terms of actual contacts these so called 'orientation processes' typically involve the highest level decision-makers in wide-ranging discussions that often take place in large, lengthy and preplanned meetings. The particular advantage of a large metropolitan centre is that it offers the variety of contact opportunities with, for instance, government officials, politicians, university and private researchers,

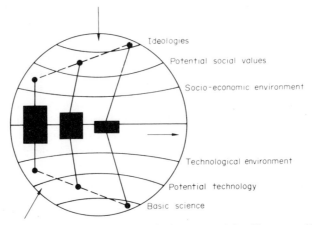

Fig. 19. Sources of information in the development space (after Thorngren, 1970)

The development space (a concept introduced by Janstch (1967) in connection with long run technological development) is divided into a values environment and a knowledge environment, with activities located in the central section. Most activities (programmed processes (1)) operate within contemporary socio-economic and technological environments. The next largest group (planning processes (2)) link potential social values and technologies and are therefore concerned with likely changes in the more immediate environments within which programmed activities currently operate. Finally, a very small proportion of total activity (orientation processes (3)) is concerned with long term scanning of the environment, reaching out to ideology and basic science.

which are essential for the conduct of these processes. Present and likely future developments in telecommunications are not likely to provide a substitute for the type of face-to-face contact activity which are vital to these processes.

Corresponding to a more immediate segment of the time horizon are processes and related information flows concerned principally with the development of specific alternatives which have been identified through the more long-term orientation processes. Such activities as research directed towards the development of specific products or projects for the intermediate future can be classified as belonging to these planning processes. As Fig. 20 suggests, information search is far more directed and less dependent on random contacts than is the case in orientation processes. Indeed, the great variety of information and contact opportunities thrown up in the city centre may conflict with the development of a specific project. Such activities could be threatened by communications overload in the metropolis (Ramstrom, 1967). In terms of contact patterns, Thorngren has shown that telecommunications are often used in planning contacts, but these need to be reinforced periodically by face-to-face meetings.

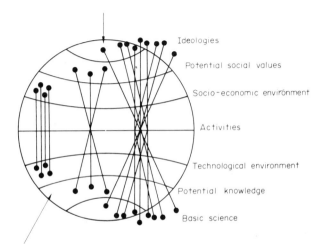

Fig. 20. Contact patterns in the development space (after Thorngren, 1970)
Orientation processes and related contacts involve a wide ranging and often random scanning of the knowledge and values environments. Planning processes give rise to contacts that take the form of a more directed evaluation and development of new possibilities isolated through previous orientation contacts. Programmed activities and contacts are severely constrained by existing arrangements, possibly laid down in earlier planning contacts.

Finally, by far the largest proportion of communications in the city centre are likely to be concerned with day-to-day control of on-going processes. The matters to be dealt with occur on a regular basis, and standardised decision procedures can be applied (Simon, 1960). These programmed processes are most suited to telecommunications because usually only a limited number of individuals are involved in each contact; as a result of the frequency of their contacts, these individuals are likely to be very familiar with one another; there is also likely to be little need for feedback or two-way exchanges of information — features which are both characteristic of orientation contacts. Theoretically there is no reason why such processes should not be carried on outside the city centre. However, the sheer volume of communications involved could make complete dispersal of these functions prohibitive on cost grounds.

This model implies that each of the different organisational processes associated with orientation, planning and programmed activities have quite different environmental demands. While orientation processes demand a very rich and diverse environment in terms of potential contact opportunities, this diversity is not so essential for the purposes of planning and programmed activities. Indeed, the possible conflicts that exist between all three processes could be heightened by common localisation within the city centre. For example, the large volume of routine contact activity associated with programmed processes could take up all of the time available and so effectively inhibit or dampen down planning activity. An unnecessary amount of office space taken up by programmed activity may also decrease that available for the more essential orientation processes, and this could lead to unwarranted increases in prices.

CONTACT PATTERNS: A MULTIVARIATE CLASSIFICATION

The immediate question now is, How appropriate is this general model of communication processes to the observed pattern of business contacts in Central London? Are there significant variations between business sectors, different types of departments and individual firms in the proportion of contacts that are of each type? The model assumes that there is an underlying or *latent* dimension to contacts, relating to the time horizon, and that the three classes of orientation, planning and programmed contacts refer to specific sections of this continuum. The object of any analysis of the contact data should be to assign each contact event to a position along this continuum and more specifically to one of the three basic classes. The individual contact data can only be related to these latent classes by way of the scores on the observed or manifest indicators which are assumed to be relevant to the latent continuum. In outlining the model a number of observed variables, such as length, number of people involved in the contact, have been hypothesised as related to the underlying dimension. Although the relevance of these particular variables can be debated, the cross-tabulations of contact characteristics have indicated such a consistent relationship between them that lends support to the notion of such a dimension. Scores of each contact on the various diary questions may therefore be used with some confidence to assign each of the contacts to one of the three hypothesised latent classes within the framework of a latent structure model. Because of the way the data is scaled, latent profile analysis (LPA) is taken as the appropriate statistical model for linking the conceptual model and the contact data.

LATENT PROFILE ANALYSIS

Latent profile analysis is a generalisation of the discrete class model of latent structure analysis to deal with the problems of identifying a latent continuum amongst continuously scaled manifest data (Gibson, 1959; Lazerfeld and Henry, 1968). In latent structure analysis the manifest data are dichotomous (yes, no) responses to a series of questions or items. In this instance it would have been possible to dichotomise the contact data — for instance on the question of prearrangement into unarranged or arranged contacts. Eight characteristics of contacts would have produced 2^8 possible patterns of responses (e.g. unarranged, short, telephone contacts, etc., etc., etc.). The purpose of latent structure analysis is then to determine the probability of an individual contact with a particular observed pattern of characteristics belonging to each latent class — or conversely the probability of a member of each of the three classes having a particular response pattern. Under the hypothesised model, a contact which was unarranged by telephone and between two people who had met before, etc., would be expected to have a high probability of belonging to the class of programmed contacts and therefore to be concerned with the immediate time horizon.

This approach would have meant abandoning a considerable amount of variation in the data. Since each of the categories into which the diary questions have been divided represents an explicit or implicit numerical ordering, the data can be treated as quantitative variables and more profitably analysed using the extension of latent structure analysis, LPA, developed by Gibson for continuous data. The basic model is the same except that the parameters relating the individual contact to the underlying or latent classes are not probabilities but average scores for each of the manifest variables over all of the members of the class.

These parameters are derived in both models on the assumption of within-class independence. For example, although relative to other classes, orientation contacts might be long and involve a large number of people, within this particular class there should be no relationship between the length of the meeting and the number of people involved. The object of the LPA, then, is to define clusters of contact in which the degree of correlation amongst the various characteristics is zero. For example, with two characteristics the correlation between the two variables would be indicated by an elongated scatter of points. The LPA seeks to identify within this scatter some sets of points which form a perfect circle, i.e. in which the two characteristics are *locally* uncorrelated. The characteristics that make such groups distinctive are identified by comparing the means and standard deviations of the members of each group with respect to the two variables with the mean and standard deviation of the whole sample. (A full statement of LPA is given in Appendix D).

For the purposes of this classification, both telephone contacts and meetings have been entered together into the analysis. Eight characteristics are common to both. These are: length, prearrangement, frequency, purpose, range of subject-matter discussed, concern with sales or purchases, number of participants and the media involved. Telephone contacts were entered through the creation of an additional variable 'media' which takes on the value 'one' for a telephone contact and 'two' for a meeting. The number of people involved in a telephone contact is coded as 'two'. For the purposes of this analysis, the scale for frequency of contact was reversed from that on the contact record sheet, so that the value 'one' equals a first contact and value 'five' equals a daily contact. The question on purpose, as categorised on the contact record sheets, could not be entered into the analysis as a quantitative variable. It was therefore recoded to indicate whether the contact involved one-way or two-way interaction – in other words whether some feedback was necessary. Orders, advice and information given and received, i.e. one-way interaction, were coded 'one', and bargaining, exchanging information and general discussion were coded 'two', i.e. two-way interaction. This variable is henceforth referred to as 'feedback'.

Three latent profiles give the best fit to this data, composed altogether of 6680 contacts. The latent profiles and the associated observed profiles are given in Table 30. 971 contacts (14.5% of the total) can be assigned to class I, the bulk (81·2%) to class II, and a small proportion (2·4%) to class III. The three observed profiles are summarised in Fig. 21, where each axis, scaled in standardised units, represents one of the original eight variables. Thus contacts in class I are characterised by having a mean length of 1·90 standard deviations above the mean length of all contacts in the sample (1·21), while those in class II are −0·37 standard deviations below the grand mean. Contacts in class I are therefore meetings of above-average length, arrangement and number of people involved; also, these contacts are concerned with above-average range of subject matter and an above-average degree of feedback.

TABLE 30. *Latent Profile Analysis: Telephone Contacts and Face-to-face Meetings*

Variable	Latent profiles			Observed profiles			Observed grand mean	Observed Discriminability
	I	II	III	I	II	III		
Media	2·00	−0·38	−0·13	1·90	−0·37	0·59	1·21	0·718
Length	2·08	−0·36	−0·52	2·01	−0·34	−0·29	1·49	0·776
Arrangement	1·86	−0·35	−0·09	1·62	−0·34	0·94	1·77	0·627
Frequency	−0·65	−0·09	2·83	−0·58	0·03	1·41	2·93	0·542
Feedback	1·10	−0·27	0·73	0·76	0·18	0·87	1·36	0·269
Range	1·02	−0·30	1·33	0·79	−0·18	0·84	1·25	0·331
Trading	0·10	0·18	−2·61	0·10	0·04	1·14	2·04	0·429
Participants	1·80	−0·30	−0·63	1·58	−0·27	−0·27	1·13	0·586
F	1016·60	5269·20	394·20	971	5429	280		
P	·152	·789	·059	14·5	81·2	4·2		

Observed and latent profile tests

Profile	A	B
1	0·542	1·12
2	0·231	0·25
3	2·490	2·06
Mean distance	1·088	

A, Distance between observed and theoretical profiles.
B, Absolute difference between sum of latent profile elements and sum of observed profile elements.

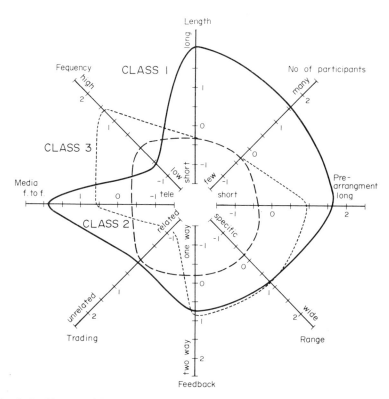

Fig. 21. A classification of face-to-face meetings and telephone contacts using LPA (three profiles).

These contacts take place with below-average frequency and hence involve generally unfamiliar participants. In complete contrast, contacts in class II are generally made by telephone, are of below-average length, arrangement and number of people involved; these contacts also have below-average feedback and are concerned with a below-average range of subject-matter. On the other hand, contacts in class II take place with above-average frequency. Class III represents a small but distinctive group. It is characterised by contacts that are generally short, very infrequent, involve only two participants, but which are arranged a long time in advance. These contacts require a fair amount of feedback and are directly concerned with sales or purchases.

The differences between observed and latent profiles are indicative of the goodness of fit of the model. Of the three profiles, profile II provides the best fit to the data and profile III the poorest fit. Of the eight variables, media, length and prearrangement are the most effective in discriminating between the three types of contact. Surprisingly, the degree of feedback is a poor discriminator between the groups.

It is possible to be more specific about the nature of the contacts in each class by examining their characteristics in terms of the original variable categories. Instead of a single figure representing the mean of all of the contacts in each class, the number of contacts falling into each of the categories of the original variables can be calculated. These frequencies are given for the contacts in each class in Table 31.

TABLE 31. *Characteristics of contacts in each class in relation to original variable categories*

	I		II		III	
	No.	%	No.	%	No.	%
Media						
Telephone	6	0·2	5093	93·8	152	54·2
F/F	965	99·8	336	6·2	128	45·7
Length						
2–10 minutes	17	1·7	4624	85·2	222	79·3
10–30 minutes	213	21·9	773	14·2	58	20·7
30–60 minutes	225	26·3	30	0·5	0	0·0
1–2 hours	268	27·6	1	0·1	0	0·0
Over 2 hours	218	22·5	1	0·1	0	0·0
Arrangement						
Unarranged	40	4·1	4455	82·1	112	40·0
Same day	98	10·1	5000	9·2	22	7·8
Day before	118	12·2	241	4·4	21	7·5
2–7 days	392	40·1	167	3·0	4	0·1
Over 1 week	323	33·2	66	1·2	121	43·2
Initiation						
Myself	526	53·7	2759	50·8	118	40·1
Other	439	45·1	2654	48·8	168	59·9
Frequency						
Daily	30	3·1	884	16·2	231	82·6
Weekly	99	10·1	1217	22·4	46	16·4
Monthly	139	14·3	787	14·4	1	0·0
Occasional	421	43·3	1915	35·2	1	0·0
First	282	29·0	625	11·5	1	0·0
Purpose						
Give order	49	0·9	730	13·4	25	8·9
Receive order	9	0·9	224	4·1	3	1·0
Give advice	48	4·9	328	6·0	6	2·0
Receive advice	33	3·3	480	8·8	1	0·3
Bargaining	72	7·4	210	3·8	119	42·5
Give information	45	4·6	851	15·6	7	2·5
Receive information	84	8·6	1335	24·9	26	6·4
Exchange information	281	28·9	812	14·9	66	23·5
General discussion	242	24·7	302	5·6	32	11·4
Other	107	11·0	153	2·8	1	0·3
Range						
One subject	461	47·5	4622	85·1	123	43·9
Several subjects	394	40·5	766	14·1	137	48·9
Wide range	116	11·9	41	0·8	17	6·1
Sales or purchases						
Directly related	284	29·2	1876	34·5	271	96·7
Indirectly	276	28·4	1284	23·7	8	2·8
Unrelated	410	42·2	2268	41·8	1	0·3

In this table the original responses to the question of purpose are given rather than the combined values for the generated variables referred to as 'feedback' in the latent profile analysis. Amongst other things, this table shows that contacts in class I are predominantly face-to-face meetings and those in class II predominantly telephone contact, although there are in the latter class a number of meetings with characteristics broadly similar to the telephone contacts that dominate the class as a whole. It is these contacts that can be described as sub-optimal, even with respect to current communications technology. Class III 'contains telephone contacts and meetings in fairly even proportions. Many of the other characteristics follow from this basic differentiation according to media. For instance, in terms of the original categories of purpose, most of the contacts in class I involve information exchanges or general discussion (53% of the total), i.e. contacts involving two-way interactions. Contacts in class II are most frequently concerned with giving or receiving information (35·5%) and also giving orders (13·4%). The biggest group of contacts in class III are those involving bargaining (42·5%).

ORIENTATION, PLANNING AND PROGRAMMED CONTACTS AND DECENTRALISATION POSSIBILITIES

On the evidence of the latent profile analysis there can be little doubt that contacts in class I can be associated with the orientation processes of the basic model. The fact that these contacts are dominated by large preplanned meetings suggests a high degree of formality in the contacts which might at first seem to run counter to the idea of 'orientation'. Nevertheless, formal occasions like large conferences often imply that a large number of people are brought together for the first time and raises the possibility of a substantial number of individuals making new acquantances. So informal connections are made possible at seemingly unproductive large meetings, and these might form the basis of more intensive and immediately productive future contacts. Orientation contacts may therefore create a necessary condition for subsequent activities by bringing together people who would not otherwise have met and raising ideas that might not otherwise have been aired. The importance of the large wide-ranging meeting for these processes also implies that future telecommunications systems are likely to be ineffective. This is because telecommunications are likely to inhibit chance connections – connections which in the long run may prove to be the most productive aspects of the large meeting in the sense that they link forward to more intensive planning activities.

Contacts in class III can be more tentatively associated with the planning processes of the basic model. These contacts are more intensive than the orientation contacts since they involve a limited number of people meeting frequently for bargaining rather than general discussion. The contacts form part of a chain in which preplanned meetings and unarranged telephone calls alternate. The existing use of telecommunications and a high degree of familiarity of participants suggest that decentralisation would be possible provided the opportunities for face-to-face contact to reinforce telecommunications were available.

Finally, contacts in class I are clearly of the programmed variety. In the main these contacts form part of a well-established contact network involving straightforward questions and answers between acquainted individuals. Also included are isolated inquiries from unknown sources. Because these contacts are predominantly by telephone they would not seriously be affected by decentralisation. Also, since programmed contacts do not form part of a communications chain (i.e. they are not closely related to previous or subsequent contact), a loss of individual connections through decentralisation would not be too serious.

There is also the possibility that many of the Central London contacts, because of their low-level nature, could be replaced in a decentralised location from local sources.

A CROSS-NATIONAL COMPARISON

Through the use of broadly similar diary survey and analysis techniques, a comparison can be made with a study of business contacts conducted by Thorngren in Stockholm in 1968. This survey included firms in three other cities, but the results presented here refer only to units located in Stockholm, not all of which were central offices. External contacts were defined as external to the building rather than external to the firm as in this study. Thorngren carried out a latent profile analysis of the data using a basically similar set of variables. In Table 32 the characteristics in raw score units of a three-profile classification of the Stockholm contact data is presented alongside the London classification. In spite of the differences between the two studies there is a high degree of similarity in the classification. In the London sample the orientation profile contains marginally more contacts arranged a long time in advance, more taking place relatively frequently, and more concerned with a wide range of general subjects. In the Swedish sample the programmed profile includes more meetings and relatively more long contacts, but is otherwise almost identical. The planning profile for Central London is distinguished from its Swedish counterpart by a large number of contacts directly concerned with sales or purchases that have been arranged well in advance.

TABLE 32. *The Classification of Business Contacts in Stockholm and London: A cross-national Comparison*

	Orientation		Planning		Programmed	
	Stockholm	London	Stockholm	London	Stockholm	London
Media	2·0	2·0	1·5	1·5	1·8	1·1
Length	3·6	3·5	1·4	1·2	1·5	1·2
Arrangement	3·0	3·9	1·2	3·0	1·4	1·3
Frequency	2·9	2·1	4·6	4·8	3·0	3·0
Range	1·9	1·6	1·8	1·7	1·2	1·2
Selling	2·2	2·1	2·7	2·1	2·1	1·0
Participants	2·0	1·9	1·1	1·0	1·1	1·0

Note: There was no comparable question on feedback in the Stockholm study. Figures are class means in raw score units, i.e. the mean score for orientation contacts for media = 2·0; all of the contacts are therefore meetings.

The similarity between the two studies lends support to the idea of a fundamental dimension underlying contact patterns that is independent of other national differences. Indeed, within Sweden, Thorngren's results for other cities (Gothenburg, Sundsvall and Umea) again yield a broadly similar classification regardless of the regional situation. The most important regional differences concern the number and proportion of contacts that are of each basic type. In particular, firms in the more peripheral regions had a much lower proportion of orientation contacts than firms in Stockholm and Gothenburg, a fact that could both be a cause and a result of low growth rates and slow adaption to change in these regions.

In this study location is a constant. Interest is therefore focused in the next chapter on differences between business sectors, departments, status groups and individual firms in the proportion of contact that are of each type. This is an important additional indicator of decentralisation opportunities.

CHAPTER 9

Variations in Contact Characteristics

INTRODUCTION

The purpose of the classification of business contacts has been to suggest the strength of inter-sectoral linkages so that decentralisation possibilities might be identified. Ideally, the delimitation of office complexes should have followed rather than preceded this classification. If there had been sufficient data it would then have been possible to search for clusters of related office activities according to all three networks. Such an approach would almost certainly have revealed that the fundamental office complexes isolated in the spatial analysis and in the analysis of aggregate information flows were dominated by programmed communication. If this were the case there would be strong grounds for arguing that close proximity is not a necessary condition for the existence of such complexes.

Such an argument is supported by a recently completed study of contacts between government agencies in Stockholm (Thorngren and Goddard, 1973). In this study separate analyses of inter-agency contact matrices for orientation, planning and programmed contact networks showed that the programmed network was the most clearly structured — as measured by the leading eigenvalues from a principal components analysis. Virtually no clusters of agencies could be identified in the orientation networks although some significant groupings of agencies were related to one another through a network of planning contacts. Examination of the geographical location of the terminal points of each type of contact within Stockholm indicated that the spatial distribution of orientation contacts was also highly dispersed while programmed contacts were confined to the immediate locality of the agency.

Because of insufficient data, inter-sectoral contacts in Central London could not be classified according to the basic model. Nevertheless, it is possible to examine variations between sectors, types of department and individual firms in the proportion of contacts of each type (particularly of the orientation variety) and so derive additional indicators of decentralisation opportunities for each of these levels of analysis.

VARIATIONS BY STATUS GROUP

Not surprisingly, individuals at the highest status level have the highest proportion of contacts associated with the orientation network (Table 33). Perhaps more significant is the fact that all groups have some contacts of each type. Even at the individual level it will probably be difficult to isolate people whose time is entirely taken up by only one type of contact activity. Nevertheless, the proportion of programmed contacts does in aggregate decrease with the increase of status. Thus, 90% of the contacts in group 5, executives, are of

TABLE 33. *Ranking of Status Groups According to Proportion of Orientation Contacts*

Group	No. of contacts	Sector contacts (%)	LPI contacts (%)	Total No. contacts	Total contacts (%)
1. Managing director, chairman, senior partner	37	19·2	3·8	193	2·9
2. Director, company secretary, junior partner	83	16·4	8·5	507	7·6
3. Manager, section head	560	15·1	57·7	3707	55·5
4. Assistant manager, section subhead, professional	207	15·8	21·0	1308	19·6
5. Executive	83	8·6	8·6	965	14·4
All status groups	970	14·5	100·0	6680	100·0

the routine variety as compared with 78% in group 2, directors, company secretaries and junior partners. Group 1 is an exception to this general relationship, with individuals having proportionately more programmed contacts than those in the group below. It follows from this relationship that the proportion of orientation contacts increases with status. Nineteen per cent of the contacts recorded by managing directors fall into class 1, compared with only 9% of contacts recorded by executives. The bulk of the planning contacts (74%) are recorded by individuals in status group 3 — managers and section heads. Planning activities are clearly, then, the function of middle management.

VARIATIONS BY TYPE OF DEPARTMENT

In Table 34 departments are arranged according to the proportion of their contacts that are of the orientation variety. Over the entire sample 14·5% of all contacts are of this type. The ranking is therefore divided into those departments above and below average — about which there is a considerable range — from 36% for computer services departments to 7% for export departments. In part these differences can be attributed to variations in the status level of sampled individuals within the department. Nevertheless, job functions associated with, for example, organisations and methods, are more likely to involve orientation contacts than jobs of equivalent status in buying or accounts. Not surprisingly, though, some of the departmenrs with the highest proportion of orientation contacts have the lowest intensity contact overall (cf. Table 22, page 165). This is simply because the length of these contacts reduces the time available for more frequently occurring, but shorter, planning or programmed contacts.

It follows, therefore, that departments with a low number of orientation contacts can have a high proportion of programmed contacts. The only exception to this are financial departments which account for the bulk of planning contacts in Central London, i.e. contacts that are short, involve only two participants, are concerned directly with buying or selling, but which are often arranged a long time in advance: 148 or 20% of all financial department contacts are of this type, representing 53% of all contacts in this class; buying, insurance and market departments also account for a significant proportion of the planning contacts.

TABLE 34. *Ranking of Departments According to Proportion of Orientation Contacts*

Department	No. of contacts	Department contacts (%)	LPI contacts (%)	Total No. contacts	Total contacts (%)
Above average					
Computer services	26	35·6	2·7	73	1·1
Miscellaneous office services	13	35·1	1·3	37	0·6
Maintenance	36	27·7	3·7	130	1·9
Organization and methods	7	25·0	0·7	28	0·4
Planning	34	22·8	3·5	149	2·2
Advertising	55	22·0	5·7	250	3·8
Personnel	90	21·0	9·3	428	6·4
Market research	12	18·8	1·2	64	1·0
Marketing	72	18·5	7·4	390	5·8
Research and development	19	17·1	2·0	111	1·7
Director and administration	150	16·7	15·4	902	13·5
Architects	13	15·9	1·2	82	1·2
Legal and patents	12	15·6	1·2	77	1·1
Technical design	10	14·9	1·0	67	1·0
Professional services	20	14·8	2·1	135	2·0
Engineers	37	14·7	3·8	252	3·8
Public relations	30	14·5	3·1	207	3·1
Below average					
Sales	43	13·0	4·4	332	5·0
Production	60	12·3	6·2	487	7·3
Property	21	11·8	2·2	178	2·7
Insurance	31	11·8	3·2	261	3·9
Information services	4	10·5	0·4	38	0·6
Client relations	6	9·3	0·6	64	0·9
Financial	69	9·2	7·1	753	11·3
Buying	42	8·8	4·3	478	7·2
Accounts	25	7·9	2·6	313	4·7
Export	17	7·1	1·8	241	3·6
Transport and distribution	1	3·4	0·1	29	0·4
Company records	0	0·0	0·0	6	0·1
All departments	971	14·5	100·0	6680	100·0

TABLE 35. *Ranking of Sectors According to Proportion of Orientation Contacts*

Sector	No. of contacts	Sector contacts (%)	LPI contacts (%)	Total No. contacts	Total contacts (%)
Above average					
Gas, electricity and water	25	26·9	2·6	93	11·4
Food, drink and tobacco	19	26·0	2·0	73	1·1
Engineering	57	20·3	5·9	281	4·2
Chemicals	224	17·6	23·1	1270	19·0
Banking	168	17·0	17·3	985	14·7
Wholesale distribution	14	16·5	1·4	85	1·3
Professional services	49	15·4	5·0	318	4·8
Paper, printing and publishing	31	13·3	3·2	203	3·0
Below average					
Transport and communications	4	14·3	0·4	28	0·4
Entertainment	47	13·5	4·8	347	5·2
Other manufacturing	48	12·9	4·9	371	5·6
Insurance	44	12·7	4·5	346	5·2
Construction	36	12·3	3·7	292	4·4
Business services	71	12·2	7·3	580	8·7
Societies and associations	32	12·0	3·3	267	4·0
Metals and other metal goods	3	10·0	0·3	30	0·4
Other finance	69	9·2	7·1	749	11·2
Primary industry	2	55·9	0·2	34	0·5
Commodity dealing	18	8·1	1·9	221	3·3
Miscellaneous offices	3	6·5	0·3	46	0·7
All sectors	971	14·5	100·0	6680	100·0

VARIATIONS BY SECTOR

In Table 35 each of the two-digit sectors is arranged according to the proportion of its total contacts assigned to the orientation profile. The sectors are again divided into those that have proportionately more profile I contacts than the average for the whole sample and those that have a below-average proportion. As in all preceding analyses by sector, the results are obviously influenced by variations in sample size. There is no clear distinction in the ranking between groups of sectors, e.g. manufacturing sectors, finance sectors or service sectors. Thus banking, with 17% of its total contact in the orientation class, is above the average figure of 14·5%, while insurance and other finance both fall below the average with 13% and 9% respectively. Professional services with an above-average share of orientation contacts are distinguished from business services with a below-average proportion. Manufacturing sectors fall into both groups, with both above- and below-average shares of this type of contact.

VARIATIONS FOR INDIVIDUAL FIRMS

In spite of problems relating to sample size it is clear that many of the traditional organisational or statistical conventions for classifying business activities are not particularly useful dimensions for differentiating contact patterns in the city centre. In fact all sectors, status groups and types of department maintain contacts falling into each of the classes. In part this may reflect the ease with which all three processes can be carried on in Central London. It follows therefore that each of the three processes must characterise individual firms although their relative importance could vary between firms.

To examine this contention, the contact data from a selection of several firms with a large sample of respondents was separately classified using latent profile analysis. In some instances, a separate planning profile could not be identified, so for comparative purposes, analyses presented here refers to a two-class classification into orientation and programmed contacts. For this analysis, the question on frequency was classified in the same way as on the contact diary (i.e. 1 = daily contact, 5 = first contact). This is the reverse of the coding used in the analyses of all contacts. Also, the question on purpose was categorised as on the diary and was not transformed to the generated variable 'feedback' used in the full analysis.

In spite of the differences in the scaling of the variables, Table 36 indicates that the classification of contacts is similar at the firm level to that derived from a large sample of individuals drawn from a number of different companies. Clearly, all firms need to maintain contact of both the programmed and the orientation variety. The table also indicates, even at the firm level, that the same regularities of contact structure exist regardless of sector. In terms of media all of the contacts in class I are face-to-face contacts. The majority of contacts in class II are made up of telephone calls although there are some exceptions. Thus the mean score for class II contacts for the clearing bank head office is 1·2, indicating that the programmed class in this instance does include a number of meetings. In terms of length of contact in class I, the property company records the lowest average length of meeting, and the oil company together with the pharmaceutical company, the highest average length of meeting. Orientation meetings are arranged furthest in advance by respondents in the oil company and with least notice in the case of the consultant civil engineers. Because the class II contacts for the head office of the clearing bank include meetings, the average score for arrangement is above that of those for other firms in this class. The lowest frequency of contact in class II is recorded by respondents in the oil company and the highest frequency by respondents in the clearing bank. The banking contacts in class II are also most likely to be related to trading.

Although there are basic similarities in the contact structure, minor differences between individual firms can be noted. The class I contacts in the oil company are most distinctively of the orientation type, while in terms of the programmed contacts the clearing bank is distinguished by having a number of meetings falling into this class. Class I contacts in the bank take place more frequently than for the other firms, and are arranged some time in advance; they are on average also more directly related to selling than the class II contacts of the other firms.

TWO CASE STUDIES

In preceding sections one of the most notable contrasts in contact characteristics has been between industrial and financial firms. On average, respondents in the industrial sectors tend to have a lower intensity of contact per head and a geographically wider

TABLE 36. *A Classification of Contacts for a Selection of Individual Firms*

	Oil company 1		Oil company 2		Rubber manufacture		Pharmaceuticals		Clearing bank head office		Property company		Civil Engineering Consultants	
	OR	PRO	OR	PRO	OR	PRO	OR	PRO	OR	PRO	OR	PRO	OR	PRO
Media	2·0	1·1	2·0	1·0	2·0	1·0	2·0	1·1	2·0	1·2	2·0	1·0	2·0	1·0
Length	3·3	1·3	4·0	1·3	3·7	1·2	4·0	1·2	3·6	1·2	3·0	1·1	3·4	1·2
Arrangement	4·2	1·4	4·4	1·3	3·8	1·3	4·0	1·3	4·0	1·9	3·6	1·2	3·0	1·2
Frequency	4·0	2·9	3·9	3·1	3·1	3·1	4·2	3·1	3·8	2·4	3·7	3·3	3·5	3·4
Purpose	7·8	5·6	8·0	6·5	7·2	6·0	7·3	5·3	7·4	5·9	8·0	5·3	6·7	6·4
Range	1·6	1·2	1·8	1·3	1·6	1·2	1·5	1·2	1·9	1·2	1·4	1·1	1·2	1·1
Trading	2·3	2·2	2·2	2·2	1·9	2·4	2·2	1·8	2·3	1·7	2·6	2·3	1·8	2·0
Participants	1·8	1·0	2·5	1·0	1·7	1·0	1·6	1·0	2·0	1·0	2·0	1·0	1·7	1·0
Total	109	360	158	121	24	185	23	116	61	427	43	313	28	209
%	23·2	76·8	23·4	76·6	13·0	87·0	16·5	83·5	14·3	85·7	13·7	86·3	11·3	88·3

Note: Figures are class means in raw score units. OR = orientation contacts. PRO = programmed contacts.

contact field than individuals from the financial sectors. If, however, the number of contacts received by each sector in the inter-sectoral analysis is respectively standardised by the total office employment in Central London in that sector, this picture is reversed. This suggests that although the sampled individuals in the manufacturing firms have fewer contacts per head than corresponding individuals in finance, when account is taken of total office employment there appears to be a much larger proportion of workers with little contact activity in the financial groups. And although respondents in the manufacturing sectors have fewer contacts per head than their counterparts in finance, these are more clearly of the orientation variety. In this section these overall differences are examined in two individual firms with approximately the same number of respondents completing diaries — one the head office of a London clearing bank and the other the head office of an international oil company.

The bank employed 9000 people at its head office, and the sample consisted of 50 individuals drawn from each of the principal departments. The oil company employed 450 people at its head office and the sample consisted of 45 individuals — again from all the principal departments. There is, therefore, a considerable difference in the sample size with the respondents in the clearing bank backed up by a much larger support staff than those in the oil company. Some 293 telephone contacts were recorded in the bank, an average of 5·8 per respondent over the 3-day period, and 338 in the oil company, an average of 7·5 per respondent. For meetings, 156 were recorded in the bank, an average of 3·1 per respondent, and 131 in the oil company, an average of 2·9 per respondent. Thus individuals in the oil company have a higher intensity of telephone contacts than those in banking, and vice versa for meetings.

The sector and geographical distribution of the telephone and meeting contacts for the two firms are given in Table 37. (Note: because meetings with more than one other person involved may include participants from a number of different sectors and regions, these additional participants are recorded in these tables as taking part in separate meetings; hence the totals of meetings are different from those quoted above.) In the case of the bank, 86% of the meetings took place with other persons working in Central London compared with 56% for the oil company. Likewise, 76% of the telephone contacts from the bank were confined to Central London, compared with 53% for the oil company. The oil company has 14% of its meetings with persons from overseas, compared with only 3% of the meetings recorded in the bank. This confirms the geographical concentration of contacts in the financial sector. Many of the subsequent differences in contact characteristics are closely related to this basic fact of the location of the other respondents in the communication.
Both firms exhibit a high degree of concentration in the sectoral distribution of their contacts. Fifty per cent of the banking meetings are with other persons in the banking sector and 54% of the oil company meetings with other firms from the chemical sector. After banking, other finance is the most significant other sector for banking meetings (24% of the total) while transport and communications is the most important external sector (11%) for the oil company. Business and professional services are minor sectors for contacts recorded in both firms. In terms of the sectoral distribution of telephone contacts, there is a marked contrast in banking from the meeting distribution, with the bulk of the telephone contacts (45%) being with other finance. Otherwise the sectoral distributions for both telephone and face-to-face meetings are broadly similar.

TABLE 37. *Sector and Geographical Distribution of Contacts for Two Firms*

Sector	FIRM A Telephone No.	%	FIRM A Meetings No.	%	Sector	FIRM B Telephone No.	%	FIRM B Meetings No.	%
Banking	32	11·1	116	50·2	Chemicals	131	39·7	111	53·6
Other finance	130	45·0	56	24·2	Transport	34	10·3	22	10·6
Business services	22	7·6	14	6·1	Professional services	33	10·0	15	7·2
Professional service	14	4·8	12	5·2	Engineering	29	8·8	10	4·8
Insurance	23	8·0	9	3·9	Business services	22	6·7	10	4·8
Paper, printing and publishing	17	5·9	4	1·7					

Regions	FIRM A Telephone No.	%	FIRM A Meetings No.	%	Regions	FIRM B Telephone No.	%	FIRM B Meetings No.	%
Central London	219	76	199	86	Central London	175	53	115	56
Greater London	37	13	12	5	Greater London	55	17	31	15
South-east Region	7	2	4	2	South-east Region	44	13	20	10
Rest of United Kingdom	25	9	10	4	Rest of United Kingdom	48	15	11	5
Overseas	1	0	6	3	Overseas	8	2	30	14
Total	289	100			Total	330	100	207	100

Note: Only sectors receiving 5% or more of all contacts from each firm are listed
Firm A: Head office of London clearing bank (50 respondents).
Firm B: Head office of oil company (45 respondents).

The characteristics of the contacts recorded in each firm are compared in Table 38, The table reveals some striking differences. Telephone contacts tend to be longer though they are not arranged so far in advance in the oil company. These are more likely to be initiated by the individual or his firm than the telephone calls in the bank. A smaller proportion of the telephone calls to and from the oil company take place on a daily basis than those in the bank.

TABLE 38. *A Comparison of Contact Characteristics for Two Individual Firms*

	Telephone		Meeting	
	Firm A	Firm B	Firm A	Firm B
	Total 293 (%)	Total 338 (%)	Total 156 (%)	Total 131 (%)
Length				
2–10 minutes	84	74	51	18
10–30 minutes	16	24	15	30
30–60 minutes	1	2	11	12
1–2 hours	0	0	15	14
Over 2 hours	0	0	7	25
Arrangement				
Unarranged	77	83	6	5
Same day	15	10	6	8
Day before	6	4	8	8
2–7 days	1	3	14	46
More than week	1	1	65	32
Initiation				
Myself	34	53	34	52
Other person	66	41	66	48
Frequency				
Daily	31	17	84	4
Once a week	25	27	7	3
Once a month	5	17	7	10
Occasional	30	29	22	54
First contact	9	10	15	28
Purpose				
Give order	7	11	2	7
Receive order	3	3	1	0
Give advice	4	11	3	12
Receive advice	9	10	2	3
Bargaining	7	1	51	4
Give information	18	12	6	2
Receive information	30	17	7	5
Exchange information	12	25	12	29
General discussion	10	8	16	12
Others	0	1	0	25
Range of subject				
One specific	75	76	70	56
Several specific	22	23	18	38
Wide range	3	1	12	6

TABLE 38 (continued)

| | Meetings Only | |
| | Firm A | Firm B |
	Total 156 (%)	Total 131 (%)
No. of people at meeting		
One other	74	56
2–4	18	30
5–10	4	9
Over 10	4	5

| | Firm A | Firm B |
	Total 38 (%)	Total 52 (%)
Meetings held outside place of work: *Method of transport*		
Walk	53	13
Bus	11	25
Private car	11	13
Taxi	5	33
Underground	18	6
Train	3	10
Plane	0	0
Length of journey		
Under 10 minutes	60	18
10–30 minutes	29	63
30–60 minutes	5	2
1–2 hours	3	8
Over 2 hours	3	10

Firm A: Head office of London clearing bank (50 respondents)
Firm B: Head office of oil company (45 respondents)

The most striking feature of the meeting recorded by the respondents in the bank are the very high frequency of their occurence – 84% take place daily, compared with only 4% of the meetings for the oil company. While occasional and new meetings are recorded in the bank, they account for only 37% of the total compared with 72% for the oil company. The corollary of this high frequency is that the bulk of the banking meetings (51%) last less than 10 minutes and only 22% over an hour – compared with 39% for the oil company. However, these frequent short meetings do appear to be arranged a long time in advance, which suggests that they are fixed meetings of specific financial markets and not associated with urgent matters cropping up at short notice. All of these characteristics suggest that many of these meetings could be carried out by telephone. However, the principal purpose of the banking meeting is for bargaining (51% of the total), which does involve two-way interaction and feedback, which is difficult to maintain using conventional telephone.

These differences are summarised in the latent profile analysis of the contacts for each firm presented in the previous sections alongside the results for five other firms. Although both firms have orientation and planning profiles, only 61 or 14·3% of the bank's contacts are assigned to the firm's orientation profile compared with 109 or 23·2% for the oil company. If we had carried out analyses of meetings only, the differences would have been more, striking, with substantially more of the banking meetings being of the programmed variety. Examination of the sectoral distribution of meetings from a latent profile analysis of all meetings supports this view: 53·8% of the meetings in the chemical sector are assigned to class I compared with 36·5% of all of the meetings for firms in the banking sector.

THE DECENTRALISATION OF FINANCIAL ACTIVITIES: SOME BASIC ISSUES FOR FUTURE RESEARCH

Although financial activities have traditionally been regarded as having a special need for a central location because of their heavy involvement in fact-to-face contacts, the preceding analysis has indicated that many of these contacts are of a highly routine nature and could easily be substituted by telecommunications. The very high frequency of these contacts on its own is not a factor that should prevent this substitution. Indeed, a comparative analysis would probably reveal the total cost for telecommunications would be less than that for face-to-face meetings, especially when account is also taken of other savings. However, certain other factors not examined in this analysis could be given as reasons preventing decentralisation through substitution. One of these is that contacts are frequently face to face in order that documents can be exchanged to confirm a transaction. However, this problem can easily be overcome by electronic document transmission facilities providing these could be accepted as valid evidence of the transaction. It is also sometimes argued that meetings take place because of reasons of personal trust, but if opportunities for regular (e.g. monthly) meetings were provided, telecommunications would be satisfactory for the intervening period. Already most contacts originating from financial departments are of the planning variety in which telephone contacts are interposed by meetings.

A final and difficult problem to overcome is that many individuals may have orientation, planning and programmed contacts in one day. Although no continuous time record was collected, it is possible that two routine contacts (that might be carried out by telecommunications from a decentralised location) could be separated by an orientation meeting, which would involve travel in the future if the individual were located outside London. It might then be impossible for the individual to have this contact. However, this sort of argument is based on the almost certainly false assumption that the same contacts will be carried out in a new location. In a before-and-after study of decentralisation, Thorngren has found that there was not so much a substitution of telecommunications for face-to-face meetings as a delegation of routine contact work to lower levels in the organisation. In other words, decentralisation leads to greater rationalisation of contact activity between individuals with one person devoting more of his time or more continuous blocks of time to one type of contact. In many respects this could lead to a more effective use of time than the continual interchanging between levels that is encouraged by the diverse contact environment of the city centre.

Many of these interesting issues concerning substitutability and decentralisation opportunities can only be answered by further analysis of the contact data, particularly at the individual level. A more rigorous approach to variations in contact activity would involve developing a classification of individual respondents, carrying forward information from the latent profile analysis of the contact data. Input to this analysis would therefore consist of 705 individuals, each characterised by a set of aggregated contact variables — including the number of orientation, planning and programmed contacts. Other possible variables to characterise each individual would include the total number of meetings recorded; total number of telephone calls; total number of new contacts by telephone and face-to-face meetings; the total time spent in meetings, on the telephone and in travelling (using the mid-point of each categorised response as a quantitative value); the total number of meetings and calls outside the individual's own sector, and the total number of meetings and calls to each region (i.e. Central London, Greater London, etc.). These data could then be subjected to a further latent profile analysis to give a direct classification of individuals in which data from the contact level is included. If more data of a quantitative nature concerning the individuals themselves, like income, age and education, were available, these could also be included in the latent profile analysis. It would then be possible to ascertain how far factors such as type of department, sector and status were important determinants of the amount and type of contact maintained by the individual.

Having classified individuals in this way it should be possible to carry forward the information on individual contact characteristics into an analysis in which the firms were the observations. In this final analysis, a direct classification of firms, characteristics of individuals and the firm itself — such as total numbers of employees and total turnover — could be included. With this sequential analysis, information from the micro-level can be carried forward into the inter-firm comparisons. Such an approach would overcome some of the aggregation problems inherent in the analysis presented here, with the next higher level of aggregation always providing the environment for the analysis of behaviour. Thus individual respondent's aggregate contacts could be analysed within a firm environment.

Conclusion

THE aim of this study has been to investigate the nature of the communication ties that appear to confine a substantial proportion of the nation's office jobs to Central London. More specifically, the question lying behind the study was: Which office activities in terms of their communication patterns most need to remain in Central London and which can be dispersed to other locations, particularly outside London and the South-east region? In other words, given that some redistribution of office employment is desirable on both economic and social grounds, can communications demands be used to discriminate between office activities seeking a Central London location?

The two approaches adopted to these questions have both indicated that a number of office activities in Central London belong to functionally and spatially linked office complexes. Thus the analysis of office location within the centre has identified a number of office types that have distinctive patterns of spatial association with other office activities. These include activities concerned with the trading and financial role of the City of London; publishing and related business services like advertising; civil engineering and other employment categories related to the construction industry; and, finally, activities relating to the clothing trade. The analysis of inter-sectoral information flows confirmed that these spatial groupings represent sets of functionally related offices. In other words, Central London contains a number of seemingly well-structured office systems in which functionally linked activities are localised in particular parts of the centre.

However, with the exception of financial activities, the employment categories that form these complexes account for only about one third of all Central London office employment — and this proportion is probably declining over time. Some publishers, advertising agencies, construction firms and consulting engineers have demonstrated an ability to move out of well-established office districts in the centre and others have dispersed from Central London as a whole (Goddard, 1967). In addition, a large proportion of the employment decentralised from London by the Location of Offices Bureau has been in financial activities, notably insurance.

When the characteristics of the communications between offices are examined — in order to assess the strength of the links tying offices into these functional complexes — the reason for this dispersal becomes clear, i.e. the office complexes identified in terms of spatial association and aggregate contact flows are principally defined by a network of very routine or programmed communications. Much of this communication is maintained entirely by telephone or by the sort of face-to-face meeting that could be readily replaced by telecommunications. On the evidence of the communication survey, over 80% of all contacts in Central London are of a type that could be readily carried on outside the centre.

Significantly, around 20% of all meetings have characteristics similar to telephone calls, i.e. short and specific discussions between two familiar people, which suggests that even without the introduction of any technology there is considerable scope for replacing face-to-face contact with existing telephone services. A further 5% of face-to-face meetings, principally associated with financial activities, could probably be replaced with telecommunications provided that document transmission facilities were available and individuals had the opportunity for regular (e.g. monthly) meetings. Only 15% of all contacts (the orientation contacts) recorded in the survey exhibit characteristics that suggest present telecommunications would be inappropriate — principally because they involve a large number of relatively unfamiliar people in wide-ranging discussions. Although such contacts account for 75% of all meetings, it is likely that only a small proportion of London's office workers are involved in these orientation activities.

Even within this last group of meetings, developments in telecommunications technology are occurring which could provide an adequate substitute, at least for some of the contacts (Goddard, 1971). These developments can basically be divided into broad- and narrow-band systems. The narrow-band systems enable a number of people to take part in audio-conferencing and also make possible the transmission of documents along a limited number of conventional telephone lines. Broad-band systems require many more telephone lines or their equivalents and are more expensive, but can cater for video-conferences. Although no questions specifically concerned with the reasons for choosing a meeting were included in this study, two recent surveys — of communications between blocks of work in the Civil Service and contacts maintained by offices decentralised from London through the Location of Offices Bureau — have both shown that the two most important reasons for the choice of a meeting were the need for a group to take part and the need to consult, exchange or sign documents (Collins, 1973; Goddard and Morris, 1973). On the basis of an extensive list of reasons for the choice of a face-to-face meeting in the Civil Service, Collins has estimated that 40% of these meetings could be satisfactorily performed by a narrow-band telecommunication system and 23% by a broad-band system — leaving about one-third of the meetings as unsubstitutable. The most difficult reason to deal with in this allocation of meetings to telecommunications is 'the need to gather background information', since this background information could be vital to the long-run outcome of the contact.

The major impediment to a technologically lead dispersal of office functions is that new technologies only slowly diffuse through the communication system. It will be a long time before all potential users are linked into a conference video system or are equipped with document transmission facilities. Initially, at any rate, developments in telecommunications are likely to have the greatest impact on communications between dispersed parts of large organisations like the Civil Service and not the inter-organisation links that have been the focus of this study. These developments will therefore encourage further partial dispersals from Central London. Because telecommunications facilities are first likely to be introduced in London and then in other large office centres, they are likely to reinforce the contact accessibility of the capital and therefore increase its attractiveness as a location for top control functions.

In concentrating solely upon the features of existing communications and adopting a purely technological approach to the strength of office linkages to the city centre, there is a danger of overlooking the organisational processes to which communications are related. It would be wrong to assume that the possibility of dispersal is solely a matter of the cost of stretching existing communication links. This is because contact patterns in any location are an expression of a complex relationship between the organisation and its 'contact environment'. By changing the organisation's access to the contact environment through dispersal, new patterns of communication will emerge. In the short run, some contacts will be maintained with Central London and others will be replaced with new contact sources; but in the long run it is highly likely that the nature of the activity itself will change in a way that will depend on how the organisation interacts with its new environment. For instance, the dispersal of high-level orientation activities to areas dominated by routine or programmed functions and lacking the intermediate planning activities necessary to develop the new possibilities that are identified by orientation processes could eventually lead to the extinguishing of the orientation activities in the new location.

The importance of the immediate locality in determining how an organisation interacts with the contact environment cannot be overemphasised. In Central London, 78% of all business journeys are to places less than 30 minutes away. Within this radius a very large number of potential orientation contacts can be made. In another location, the same length of journey is likely to encompass fewer and less information-rich contact sources; yet even outside the centre, contact patterns still seem to be dominated by the immediate locality. Thorngren's survey of firms located in smaller cities in the north of Sweden, as well as in Stockholm and Gothenburg, has demonstrated that 76% of all contacts are with places less than 30 minutes away. The success of a dispersal policy therefore depends as much upon the existing occupational and industrial structure of the new locations as upon their connections to the national communication system. The reluctance of firms to move to development areas — including major cities like Manchester and Newcastle — should not be seen solely in terms of problems of communications with London but also in the context of the relatively poor local contact environment. This is partly expressed in terms of an occupational structure dominated by low-level clerical and manual jobs and office centres lacking the dense network of interrelated office functions that characterise the city centres of national capitals.

Before proceeding to examine the policy implications of these findings it is appropriate to raise a number of wider issues concerning the goals and implementation of a policy of office dispersal in London. It is only slowly being appreciated by researchers and policy makers that the present distribution of office occupations is an important source of regional inequalities in both social and economic development. Because the office function can only be defined in terms of the jobs that individuals perform and not by the product of the industry in which they work, regional analysts are being forced to devote some attention to the relationship between occupational structure and development at the expense of a previously overwhelming concern with the influence of industrial structure. The occupational structure of a local labour market is important in a social context because it determines the amount of occupational and therefore social mobility which is possible without migration; in an economic context, occupational structure is important because it is related to the nature of local contact possibilities. An area dominated by predominantly low-level clerical and manual jobs would, on the one hand, provide few opportunities for occupational mobility without migration and, on the other hand, offer few contact possibilities without long journeys to new office activities. With the bulk of the national employment increase being in the form of new office-based occupations that are concentrated in London and the South-east, it is not surprising that during the period 1961-6, the net migration balance of economically active population to this region from the rest of the country was dominated by office workers (39,000 out of a total of 41,000). It is both a cause and a consequence of the concentration of office occupations in this region that office employers are reluctant to move a great distance from London.

A policy of office dispersal will therefore only be successful if it forms part of a co-ordinated effort to up-grade the quality of local contact environments in the development areas. The evidence of the communication survey presented here suggests that there is considerable potential for dispersal of routine activities if adequate telecommunications are provided *and* the communication bill can be met. Because it is primarily the lower office grades that are involved in routine contact activity, such a dispersal will, however, do little to change the character of the receiving locality — viewed both from the point of view of job opportunities for individuals and contact possibilities for firms. On the other hand, dispersal of higher level function will cause considerable communication damage if these are directed to a large number of different locations within the development areas, since these areas will inevitably provide inadequate local contact opportunities.

Probably the only way to foster dispersal and local growth of high status office jobs in the development areas in order to improve the social and contact environment, is to concentrate office development in a number of major centres well connected to the national communication system. With a sufficiently large pool of related office activities, centres like Leeds, Manchester, and Newcastle could develop the sort of office complexes that are at present only found in London and all other national capitals (e.g. Bannon, 1972; Croft, 1969). Such office complexes would offer external economies to other activities and foster the growth of new offices locally. Benefits would accrue also to industrial enterprises that would no longer have to look to London for information. Indeed, the introduction of high-level information sources at strategic points in the development areas could create the necessary conditions for growth and change that are at present lacking, possibly because of limited local contact opportunities.

The object of policy should therefore be to use key office activities as 'development poles' in peripheral regions (Hermansen, 1968, 1972). As Hermansen has pointed out, service activities in general and basic office activities in particular, can be important agents for bringing about economic development. A nucleus of offices, perhaps based in a number of major contact sources, such as government department or the head office of a national or international company, could provide the stimulus for new economic activity as well as growth and change in existing activities. Once critical contact sources have been established, functionally linked activities are likely to develop in the immediate vicinity. On an intra-urban scale, for instance, the decentralisation of one or two key civil engineering companies to the London suburban centre of Croydon led to the establishment of a civil engineering complex there, including architects, surveyors and consultants.

How can such a policy objective be achieved? The identification of a number of real alternative national office centres to London clearly needs to be seen as part of a national urban development strategy which could act as a framework for various investment decisions, including the assessment of locational priorities. The dispersal of large sections of government employment from London, including top-level jobs, could provide the necessary impetus for the growth of such alternative office centres. As the communication survey has shown, government departments are an important source of contact for commercial offices; government dispersal would encourage some London offices to follow suit and would also lead to the establishment of new office activities in the reception centres to meet the new demands.

The success of this policy would also depend on the careful dispersal and local encouragement of appropriate commercial office activities. This implies a more rigorous assessment of locational priorities for offices than is possible through present physical control of office development (Office Development Permits). One solution would be a location executive that could collect hard evidence from large office employers in London concerning, amongst other things, the strength of their communication ties to the capital. This would involve the location executive in organising communication surveys of individual organisations of the type carried out for this study. This information could be used in advising firms as to the best location for various parts of their activities within the framework of government policy. The fact that only 400 establishments account for one-third of Central London commercial office employment suggests that an executive with real power could effect a considerable dispersal of office employment.

If dispersal formed part of a positive programme of developing alternative office centres containing linked activities, it would not necessarily follow that costs would increase for individual organisations. Indeed, re-location could be used to bring about a greater rationalisation of activities within a large organisation through the location of different parts in appropriate contact environments.

In London restrictions would need to be selectively applied on those individual office activities which were not likely to add to the diversity of the capital's contact environment. In the alternative office centres, specific rather than general incentives would be required to attract in or encourage the new establishment of the type of office activities that would contribute towards the development of the local contact environment — such as certain specialist services that are required to make up a particular office complex. In applying controls in London, care would also need to be taken that dispersal of the employment does not create a temporary shortage of the type of office occupation necessary to maintain a socially diverse environment within the capital (Evesey, 1972).

These policy suggestions involve sweeping changes, particularly in terms of the replacement of physical controls in the form of Office Development Permits by a location executive with powers to steer specific office activities from one area to another through the use of fiscal controls and incentives. They also imply a commitment to a co-ordinated effort to concentrate office employment in a limited number of large centres in the development areas that have an adequate physical, social and contact infra-structure. Unless such far-reaching changes in government policy that take account of the influence of contact possibilities on regional development are implemented, the existing spiral of over-concentration will continue. Indeed, investment in communications infra-structure, such as conference video facilities and advanced passenger trains that are unco-ordinated with location policy, are only likely to increase regional differentials in contact opportunities and ultimately economic and social development.

Coding of Establishments from OSRP Registrations

			SIC
01	**PRIMARY INDUSTRY**		
	010	*Agriculture, forestry and fishing*	
		0100 Agriculture, forestry and fishing	001-003
	011	*Mining and quarrying*	
		0110 Coal mining	101
		0111 All other mining and quarrying	102, 103, 109
02	**FOOD, DRINK AND TOBACCO**		
	020	*Food*	
		0200 Cereal products	211, 213
		0201 Bacon curing, meat products	214
		0202 Fish and fish products	214
		0203 Dairy products	215
		0204 Sugar and confectionery	216, 217
		0205 Fruit and vegetables	218
		0206 Any other food industries	219, 229
	021	*Brewing and other drink industries*	
		0210 Brewing and other drink industries	231, 239
	022	*Tobacco*	
		0220 Tobacco	
03	**CHEMICALS AND ALLIED INDUSTRIES**		
	030	*Fuel and Oil*	
		0300 Fuel and oil	261-263
	031	*Chemicals*	
		0310 Chemicals, dyes, explosives	271, 273
		0311 Pharmaceuticals and toilet preparations	272
		0312 Paint and printing ink	274
		0313 Vegetable and animal oils, soap, detergents	275
		0314 Synthetic resins, plastics, polishes and adhesives	276, 277
04	**METALS AND OTHER METAL GOODS**		
	040	*Metal manufacture*	
		0400 Iron and steel, steel tubes, iron castings	311-313
		0401 Other metal manufactures	321, 322
	041	*Metal goods*	
		0410 Metal goods	391-395
		0411 Jewellery, etc.	396
		0412 All other metal industries	399

H

09 CONSTRUCTION

    090 *General construction and contracting*

	0900 General building contractors	500
	0901 Highway construction and repair	500
	0902 Heavy structural and civil engineering	500

    091 *Specialist contracting*

	0910 Plumbing, heating, air conditioning	500
	0911 Electrical contracting	500
	0912 Masonry, stonework, tiling, etc..	500
	0913 Concrete	500
	0914 Other specialist contracting including plant hire	500

10 GAS, ELECTRICITY AND WATER

    100 *Gas, electricity and water*

	1000 Gas electricity and water	601-603

11 TRANSPORT AND COMMUNICATIONS

    110 *Transport*

	1100 Railways	701
	1101 Road passenger transport	702
	1102 Road haulage	703
	1103 Sea transport	704
	1105 Air transport	706

    111 *Postal services and telecommunications*

	1110 Postal services and telecommunications	707

    112 *Transport services*

	1120 Shipping and forwarding, freight broking, etc.	709 (1)
	1121 Travel agents	709 (1)
	1122 Other transport services	709 (1)
		709 (3)

    113 *Storage associated with transport*

	1130 Storage associated with transport including bonded warehouses	709 (2)

12 WHOLESALE DISTRIBUTION

    120 *Food wholesaling*

	1200 Grocery and provisions	810 (1)
	1201 Meat and meat products	810 (2)
	1203 Fresh fruit and vegetables	810 (2)
	1204 Dairy produce	810 (2)
	1205 Other food products	810 (2)

    121 *Clothing and footwear wholesaling*

	1210 Clothing and footwear wholesaling	810 (4)

    122 *Paper, stationery and books wholesaling*

	1220 Paper, stationery and books wholesaling	810 (5)

    123 *Machinery and equipment wholesaling*

	1230 Electrical goods	810 (7)
	1231 Hardware, plumbing and heating equipment	810 (7)
	1232 Office machinery and equipment – supplies and service	810 (7)
	1233 Other commercial and professional machinery and equipment	810 (7)

    124 *Drugs, chemicals and other non-food goods wholesaling*

	1240 Drugs, chemicals and allied products	810 (7)
	1241 Other non-food goods wholesaling	810 (7)

    125 *General wholesale merchants*

	1250 General wholesale merchants	810 (8)

13   RETAIL DISTRIBUTION

  130   *Food shops*
    1300   Grocery and provisions shops   820 (1)
    1302   Other food shops   820 (2)

  131   *Confectionery, tobacco and newspapers*
    1310   Confectionery, tobacco and newspapers   820 (3)

  132   *Clothing and footwear shops*
    1320   Footwear   820 (4)
    1321   Men's and boys' outerwear   820 (4)
    1322   Other men's wear shops   820 (4)
    1323   Women's outerwear   820 (4)
    1324   Other women's wear, drapery and general clothing shops   820 (4)

  133   *Furniture and furnishing shops*
    1330   Household furniture   820 (5)
    1331   Soft furnishings   820 (5)
    1332   Floor covering   820 (5)
    1333   Antiques and second-hand furniture   820 (5)
    1334   Art dealers and galleries   820 (5)

  134   *Electrical and cycle shops and ironmongers*
    1340   Radio and electrical including hire   820 (5)
    1341   Cycles and perambulators   820 (5)
    1342   Ironmongery and hardware   820 (5)

  135   *Booksellers and stationers*
    1350   Booksellers and stationers   820 (6)

  136   *Chemists and photographic goods shops*
    1361   Chemists   820 (6)
    1362   Photographic goods shops   820 (6)

  137   *Jewellery, sports and leather goods shops*
    1370   Jewellery, watch and clock shops   820 (6)
    1371   Sports goods   820 (6)
    1372   Leather goods   820 (6)
    1373   Toy shops   820 (6)
    1374   Fancy goods and gifts   820 (6)

  138   *Other non-food goods shops*
    1380   Other non-food goods shops   820 (6)

  139   *Department and variety goods stores*
    1390   Department and variety goods stores   820 (6)

14   COMMODITY DEALING

  140   *Export and import merchants*
    1400   Export and import merchants   832

  141   *Commodity brokers, merchants and dealers*
    1410   Grain merchants   832
    1411   Metal brokers and dealers   832
    1412   Tea and coffee merchants   832
    1413   General produce merchants   832
    1414   Plantation house commodity dealers   832
    1415   Wool and fur dealers   832
    1416   Diamond merchants   832
    1417   Timber merchants   832
    1418   Miscellaneous commodity brokers   832

15   INSURANCE

  150   *Insurance companies*
    1500   Life insurance companies   860 (1)
    1501   Fire, marine and other casualty insurance   860 (1)

	151	*Other insurance*	
		1502 Life and casualty insurance combined	860 (1)
		1510 Insurance brokers	860 (1)
		1511 Underwriters and underwriters' agents	860 (1)
		1512 Other insurance – re-insurance, insurance adjusting, etc.	860 (1)

16 BANKING

	160	*Central banking*	
		1600 London clearing banks – Head offices	860 (2)
		1601 London clearing banks – other special departments	860 (2)
		1602 Merchants banks	860 (2)
		1603 Bill discounting and foreign exchange	860 (2)

	161	*Other banking*	
		1610 Other banks	860 (2)
		1611 London clearing banks – branches	860 (2)

17 OTHER FINANCE

	170	*Stockbroking and jobbing*	
		1700 Stockbroking and jobbing	860 (3)

	171	*Other Finance*	
		1710 Building societies	860 (3)
		1711 Investment and credit banks	860 (3)
		1712 Other finance	860 (3)

	172	*Property*	
		1720 Property owning and developing companies	860 (4)
		1721 Estate agents, surveyors and valuers	860 (4)

18 PROFESSIONAL AND SCIENTIFIC SERVICES

	180	*Accounting, auditing and bookkeeping*	
		1800 Accounting, auditing and bookkeeping	871

	181	*Legal services*	
		1810 Legal services	873

	182	*Consulting engineers*	
		1820 Consulting engineers	879 (1)

	183	*Architects*	
		1830 Architects	879 (1)

	184	*Management, production, marketing and costing consultants*	
		1840 Management, consultants	879 (1)
		1841 Production and costing consultants	879 (1)
		1842 Marketing consultants and market research	879 (1)

	185	*Other specialist consultants*	
		1850 Other specialist consultants	879 (1)

	186	*Educational services*	
		1860 Educational services – including language and secretarial schools	872

	187	*Medical services*	
		1870 Medical services	874

	188	*Non-profit educational and scientific research institutes and agencies*	
		1880 Non-profit educational and scientific research institutes and agencies	879

19 BUSINESS SERVICES

	190	*Advertising and public relations*	
		1900 Advertising agencies	899 (6)
		1901 Advertising services	899 (6)
		1902 Public relations consultants	899 (6)

191	*Office services*	
	1910 Typewriting and duplicating, photocopying	899 (6)
	1911 Direct mail advertising circular services	899 (6)
	1912 Translating services	899 (6)
	1913 Calculating services	899 (6)
	1914 Electronic data processing services	899 (6)
	1915 Employment agencies	899 (6)
	1916 General services to buildings	899 (6)
	1917 Security services	899 (6)
192	*Drawing and photographic services*	
	1920 Drawing services, drawing office	899 (6)
	1921 Commercial photographic services	899 (2)
193	*Miscellaneous business services*	
	1930 News agencies and press services	988 (6)
	1931 Equipment rental and leasing services	899 (6)
	1932 Other business services	899 (6)

20   SOCIETIES AND ASSOCIATIONS

200	*Employers' and trade associations*	
	2000 Employers' and trade associations	899 (6)
201	*Professional membership organisations*	
	2010 Professional membership associations	899 (6)
202	*Trade unions and labour organisations*	
	2020 Trade unions and labour organisations	
203	*Religious organisations*	
	2030 Religious organisations	875
204	*Charitable organisations*	
	2040 Charitable organisations	899 (6)
205	*Political organisations*	
	2050 Political organisations	899 (6)
206	*Other societies, associations*	
	2060 Other societies, associations	899 (6)

21   PERSONAL SERVICES

210	*Launderies, dry cleaning, shoe repair*	
	2100 Laundries, dry cleaning, shoe repair	885, 886, 888
211	*Hairdressing, barbers and beauty shops*	
	2110 Hairdressing, barbers and beauty shops	889
212	*Garages, car distributors, car hire*	
	2120 Garages, car distributors, car hire	887
213	*Other personal services*	
	2130 Other personal services	899 (1) (9)

22   ENTERTAINMENT

220	*Cinemas*	
	2200 Cinemas	881 (1)
	2201 Film producers	881 (1)
	2202 Film distributors	881 (1)
	2203 Other cinema services	881 (1)
221	*Theatres*	
	2210 Theatres	881 (2)
	2211 Theatre ticket agencies	881 (2)
	2212 Theatrical production and services	881 (2)

APPENDIX B

An Example of the Size Distribution of Establishments for Different Office Employment Categories within a sector: Other Finance

	1-10	11-25	26-50	51-100	101-150	151-250	250+	Total	Per cent Employment in Sector	Mean size of Establishment
Stockbroking and jobbing	633 (3·8) 134	1939 (11·7) 109	2951 (17·8) 78	5268 (31·8) 76	2698 (16·3) 22	2185 (13·2) 11	868 (5·2) 3	16,542 427	41·3	38·7
Building societies	213 (10·0) 40	344 (16·2) 19	553 (25·9) 15	224 (10·5) 3	0 0	183 (8·6) 1	675 (31·7) 1	2,192 79	5·5	26·9
Investment and credit banks	148 (6·9) 38	263 (12·3) 14	139 (6·5) 44	53 (2·6) 1	144 (6·7) 1	0 0	1204 (56·5) 2	1,953 60	4·9	32·5
Other finance	663 (12·6) 146	733 (14·0) 45	925 (17·6) 24	1188 (22·7) 16	256 (4·9) 2	616 (11·6) 3	850 (16·2) 2	5,231 238	13·0	29·9
Property owning and development	1048 (22·3) 266	1128 (24·0) 69	1073 (22·9) 31	987 (21·0) 15	134 (2·9) 1	320 (6·8) 2	0 0	4,690 384	11·7	12·2
Estate agents and valuers	1959 (20·6) 415	2466 (26·0) 154	1910 (20·1) 53	1942 (20·4) 28	368 (3·8) 3	836 (8·8) 5	0 0	9,481 658	23·6	14·4
Total	4664 (11·6) 1039	6873 (17·1) 410	7551 (18·8) 205	9664 (24·1) 133	3600 (8·9) 29	4140 (10·3) 22	3597 (8·9) 8	40,089	100·0	

Note: Figures give total employment, per cent total employment in the category in each size group and number of establishments.

Source: OSRP data

224

Within- and Between-sector Measures of Spatial Association

Sector	Within-sector associations (four-digit)			Between-sector associations (three-digit)		
	Four-digit category	Associations with	r	Three-digit category	Associations with	r
Primary industry				Agriculture – forestry, fishing	Commodity brokers	0·72
					Other food industries	0·56
					Wholesale merchants	0·51
					Metal manufacture	0·79
Food, drink and Tobacco				Food	Commodity brokers	0·66
					Wholesale merchants	0·34
				Tobacco	Political organisations	0·96
					Religious organisations	0·62
					Chemicals	0·52
Metals				Metal goods	Timber-furniture	0·52
Engineering	Office machinery	Industrial machinery	0·60	Heavy machinery	Specialist contracting	0·57
	Other mechanical engineering	Shipbuilding	0·81	Precision engineering	Specialist contracting	0·57
				Mechanical engineering	Accounting	0·57
					Paper	0·53
				Vehicles	Property	0·52
Textiles, leather and clothing	Textile manufacture	Made-up textiles	0·53	Clothing and footwear	Clothing and footwear, wholesale	0·82
		Fur	0·65		Drawing and photo-graphic services	0·63
		Dresses	0·53		Management consultation	0·52
	Made-up textiles	Fur	0·71	Textiles	Clothing and footwear	0·80
		Womens tailoring	0·78			
		Dresses	0·76			
		Other clothing	0·76			
		Footwear	0·76			

Sector	Within-sector associations (four-digit)			Between-sector associations (three-digit)		
	Four-digit category	Associations with	r	Three-digit category	Associations with	r
	Leather	Dresses	0·62			
		Other clothing	0·52			
		Footwear	0·66			
	Women's tailoring	Dresses	0·74			
		Other clothing	0·64			
		Footwear	0·72			
	Dresses	Other clothing	0·81			
	Dresses, etc.	Footwear	0·96			
	Other clothing	Footwear	0·79			
Paper, printing and publishing				Paper and paper products	Mechanical engineering	0·53
					Shipbuilding	0·52
				Printing and publishing	Advertising and public relations	0·56
					Drawing and photographic services	0·55
					Miscellaneous business services	0·55
Construction				Specialist contracting	Precision engineering	0·57
					Heavy machinery	0·57
Transport and communications	Sea transport	Postal services and telecommunications	0·88	Transport	Other insurance	0·59
		Shipping and forwarding	0·91	Postal services and telecommunications	Other insurance	0·76
		Shipping and forwarding	0·83		Other banking	0·59
	Postal services and telecommunications			Transport services	Other insurance	0·91
					General wholesale merchants	0·65
					Food wholesalers	0·54
					Other banking	0·51
				Transport storage	Food wholesalers	0·62
Wholesale distribution	Other food products wholesaling	General wholesale merchants	0·60	Food wholesaling	Export and import	0·63
					Other insurance	0·54
					Commodity brokers	0·50
				Clothing and footwear	Drawing and photographs	0·58

				Paper, stationery and books		Miscellaneous business services
Commodity dealing	Export and import merchants	Grain merchants	0·54	Paper, stationery and books		services 0·51
		Metal brokers	0·51	Drapery, chemicals and other non-food goods		Export and import 0·63
		Miscellaneous brokers	0·51	General wholesale merchants		Other insurance 0·50
	Grain merchants	Plantation house	0·99			Commodity brokers 0·75
		Tea and coffee merchants	0·66	Export and import merchants		Other insurance 0·64
		Metal brokers	0·64			Agriculture 0·56
		Miscellaneous brokers	0·62	Commodity brokers		Food manufacture 0·55
	Metal brokers	Tea and coffee merchants	0·66			Accountancy 0·58
		Plantation house	0·56			Head Office overseas firms 0·53
	Plantation house	Miscellaneous brokers	0·62			Office services 0·52
						Other insurance 0·77
						Head Office overseas firms 0·56
						Insurance companies 0·54
Insurance	Fire, marine and casualty insurance	Insurance brokers	0·85	Insurance companies		Other banking 0·88
		Re-insurance	0·76			Central banking 0·85
		Underwriters	0·72			Stockbroking 0·74
	Insurance brokers	Re-insurance, etc.	0·78			Legal services 0·74
		Underwriters	0·77			Accountancy 0·71
	Underwriters	Re-insurance, etc.	0·92	Other insurance		Other insurance 0·71
						Other banking 0·61
Banking	Clearing banks head office	Clearing banks departments	0·82	Central banking		Stock broking 0·88
		Other banks	0·69			Other finance 0·72
		Bill discounting and foreign exchange	0·52			Accountancy 0·58
	Clearing banks departments	Other banks	0·93	Other banking		Legal services 0·51
		Bill discounting and foreign exchange	0·82			Stock broking 0·70
						Accountancy 0·65
						Other finance 0·60
						Legal services 0·58

Sector	Within-sector associations (four-digit)			Between-sector associations (three-digit)		
	Four-digit category	Associations with	r	Three-digit category	Associations with	r
	Merchant banks	Bill discounting and foreign exchange	0·54			
	Bill discounting and foreign exchange	Other banks	0·96			
Other finance				Stockbroking	Accountancy	0·69
				Other finance	Accountancy	0·63
					Legal services	0·51
Professional and scientific services	Accounting	Legal services	0·69	Accounting	Head Office overseas	0·59
				Architect	Advertising and public relations	0·59
				Management Consultants	Professional associations	0·51
					Drawing and photographic services	0·63
Business services	Advertising agencies	Public relations	0·65			
	Advertising services	Employment agencies	0·60			
	Typing, duplicating and photocopying	Circulatory services	0·64			
	Employment agencies	Drawing services	0·51			
	Commercial photography	New agencies	0·64			
Societies and associations	Employers and trade associations	Charities	0·53			
	Political organisations	Religious organisations	0·64			

Only correlation coefficients greater than 0·50 are shown
Between-sector associations are only entered once in the table for the first-occurring sector.

APPENDIX D

Latent Profile Analysis

IN THE discrete class model of latent structure analysis (LSA), the population is assumed to be clustered into homogeneous latent classes: the division is not directly observable. The manifest or observable data are the proportions of the population who possess particular characteristics and combinations of characteristics. Thus p_i is the proportion of the population with characteristic i, p_{ij} is the proportion with characteristic i and j, and p_{ijk} the proportion with i, j and k. The latent parameters are the relative size classes: $v^1, v^2, \ldots v^q$ (where v is the proportion of the population in each of the q latent classes) and the probability of an individual i in a given class x possessing a particular characteristic p_i^x.

An assumption of local independence is made. In other words, within a particular class the possession of any characteristic is independent of the possession of any other characteristic. The equations relating manifest and latent parameters are:

$$1 = \sum_x v^x .$$

$$p_i = \sum_x v^x p_i^x \qquad \text{for all } i,$$

$$p_{ij} = \sum_x v^x p_i^x p_j^x \qquad \text{for all } i, j,$$

$$p_{ijk} = \sum_x v^x p_i^x p_j^x p_k^x \qquad \text{for all } i, j, k$$

Σ over all q latent classes.

The first equation sums to one since the terms are the proportionate sizes of each class and all individuals are discretely assigned to a class; the second defines the proportion of individuals in each of the classes possessing characteristic i; the third, the proportion in each class possessing i and j, and so on.

A variety of solutions for the latent parameters v^x, p_i^x have been suggested (Anderson, 1954; Green, 1951). On the basis of the actual pattern of characteristics an individual can be assigned to the class to which it most probably belongs. Thus with four characteristics and two classes, an individual with the pattern $(0,1,0,1)$ might have a 0.8 probability of belonging to class I and a 0.2 probability of belonging to class II.

Gibson has shown that the latent class model can be generalised to consider quantitative variables (Gibson, 1959). With q quantitative characteristics of N individuals, individual i's score on variable j would be $Y_{j, i}$. The mean score on variable j is $\overline{Y}_j$ and the variance

$$(s_j)^2 = \frac{1}{N} \Sigma_i (Y_{j,i} - \overline{Y}_j)^2$$

The raw scores must be standardized to have zero mean and unit variance:

$$Z_{j,i} = (Y_{j,i} - \overline{Y}_j) / s_j$$

The following equations then define the manifest parameters of the latent profile model:

$$\frac{1}{N} \Sigma_i Z_{j,i} = m_j = 0,$$

$$\frac{1}{N} \Sigma_i Z_{j,i} Z_{k,i} = r_{jk},$$

(2)

$$\frac{1}{N} \Sigma_i Z_{j,i} Z_{k,i} Z_{m,i} = r_{jkm},$$

Σ over all N individuals.

r_{jk} is simply the product moment correlation between variables j and k, and r_{jkm} is the average triple product or third-order correlation. The model therefore uses the same manifest parameters as factor analysis with the addition of higher order correlations like r_{123}.

As with the latent structure model, the population of individuals is assumed to be divided into several homogeneous groups. In this case the latent parameters are v^x, the relative size of class x; m_j^x, the average standard score on variable j for member of class x. The equations are, therefore,

$$
\begin{aligned}
1 \quad &= \quad \Sigma_x v^x, \\[2mm]
m_j \quad &= \quad 0 \quad = \quad \Sigma_x v^x m_j^x, \\[2mm]
r_{jk} \quad &= \quad \Sigma_x v^x m_j^x m_k^x, \\[2mm]
r_{ijk} \quad &= \quad \Sigma_x v^x m_j^x m_k^x m_i^x,
\end{aligned}
$$

(3)

Again the proportions in each class sum to one; the sum of the within-class means defines the grand mean of each variable, which for standard scores is zero; the products of within-class means, summed over all classes, define the observed inter-correlations between the variables.

The equations of LSA were derived on the assumption of within-class independence. The same assumption must be made to derive the LPA equations, with each class being homogeneous in the sense that the intercorrelations between the variables observed over the group members are all zero. Since eqns (3) are identical with those of LSA (1), the same solutions for the parameters can be applied. We have used Green's solution and a programme supplied by Mardberg (Mardberg, 1967).

The assignment of individuals to classes is different in LPA from LSA since the parameters are means and not probabilities. One solution is to assign the individuals to classes to which these are nearest in Euclidean space. In an m-characteristic space, each individual would be located according to its observed Z score on all the m variables. Each latent class can be located according to its standardized means on the m variables and every individual assigned to the nearest class. This assignment will only be approximately accurate. The observed standardised means and standard deviations of the individuals in each class can be used to define the *observed profile*. The observed within-class intercorrelations should be zero, but this may not be the case due to the possibility of mis-allocation.

Measures of goodness of fit of the classification are given by the differences between latent and observed profiles. These include a low Euclidean distance between the observed and latent profile means. Another goodness of fit criterion is low within-class standard deviations. An index measuring how effectively each variable discriminates between the individuals in each group can be defined for both observed and latent profile as:

$$
\begin{aligned}
D_i &= \quad \overset{k}{\underset{s=1}{\Sigma}} \, V_s X_i^2, \\[2mm]
x_i &= \quad \text{latent/observed profile element for variable } i, \\[2mm]
v_s &= \quad \text{proportion of individuals belonging to profile } s, \\[2mm]
k &= \quad \text{number of profiles.}
\end{aligned}
$$

All these criteria can be used to define the number of latent classes that best describe the date. This can be automatically defined when no individuals can be assigned to a particular latent class because all are nearer to one of the other classes.

References

ALEXANDER, I. C. (1972) Multivariate techniques in land use studies: the case of information analysis, *Regional Studies* 6, 93-103.

ANDERSON, T. W. (1954) On the estimation of parameters in latent structure analysis, *Psychometrika* 19, 151-66.

ANDERSON, J. (1971) Space-time budgets and activity studies in urban geography and planning, *Environment and Planning* 3, 353-68.

BACHI, R. (1962) Standard distance measures and related measures in spatial analysis, *Regional Science Association Papers* 10, 83-132.

BAKER, L. L. H. and GODDARD, J. B. (1972) Inter-sectoral contact flows and office location in Central London, in Wilson, A. G. (ed.), *London Studies in Regional Science*, vol. 3, Pion, London.

BANNON, M. (1972) *Office location in Ireland: the role of central Dublin,* National Institute for Physical Planning and Construction Research, Dublin (mimeo).

BERRY, B. J. L. (1966) *Commodity flows and the spatial structure of the Indian economy,* Department of Geography, Research Paper 111, University of Chicago.

BRAMS, S. J. (1966) Transaction flows in the international system, *American Political Science Review* 60, 880-98.

COWAN, P. *et al* (1969) *The office: a facet of urban growth.* Heinemann, London.

COLLINS, H. (1973) *The telecommunications impact models, stages I and II,* Communications Studies Group, University College, London (mimeo).

CONNELL, S. (1972) *A review of communications survey methodologies,* Communications Studies Group, University College London (mimeo).

CROFT, M. (1969) *Offices in a regional centre: follow up studies of infrastructure and linkages,* Research Paper 3, Location of Offices Bureau, London.

DAVIES, D. M. (1965) *Land use in central Capetown,* Longmans, Capetown.

DUNCAN, O. D., CUZZON, P. and DUNCAN, B. (1961) *Statistical geography: problems of analyzing areal data,* Free Press, Glencoe.

DUNNING, J. H. and MORGAN, E. V. (1971) *An economic study of the City of London,* Allen and Unwin, London.

ELTON, M. *et al* (1970) *An approach to the location of government,* Institute of Management Science, London (mimeo).

EVERSLEY, D. E. C. (1972) Old cities, falling populations and rising costs (Greater London Council Intelligence Unit), *Quarterly Bulletin* 18, 5-17.

GARRISON, W. L. and WORRAL (1968) *Monitoring urban travel,* Transportation Centre, Northwestern University, Evanston, Illinois (mimeo).

GIBSON, W. A. (1959) Three multivariate models: factor analysis, latent structure analysis and latest profile analysis, *Psychometrika* 24, 54-76.

GODDARD, J. B., (1966) The internal structure of London's Central Area, in M. van Hulten, (ed.), *Urban core and inner city,* Brill, Leiden.

GODDARD, J. B. (1967) Changing office location patterns in Central London, *Urban Studies* 4, 276-85.

GODDARD, J. B. (1968) Multivariate analysis of office location patterns in the city centre: a London example, *Regional Studies* 2, 69-85.

GODDARD, J. B. (1970a) Greater London Development plan: Central London, a key to strategic planning, *Area* 3, 52-54.

GODDARD, J. B. (1970b) Functional regions within the city centre: a study by factor analysis of taxi flows in Central London, *Transactions and Papers, Institute of British Geographers* 49, 161-82.

GODDARD, J. B. (1971) Office communications and office location: a review of current research, *Regional Studies* 5, 263-80.

GODDARD, J. B. and MORRIS, D.(1973) *Communications in decentralized offices,* Location of Offices Bureau, London (mimeo, forthcoming).

GREATER LONDON COUNCIL (1970) *Greater London development plan statement.*

GRAVES, D. (1972) Reported communication ratios and informal states in managerial work groups, *Human Relations* 25, 159-70.

GREEN, B. F. (1951) A general solution for the latent class model of latent structure analysis, *Psychometrika* 16, 151-66.

HEDBERG, B. (1969) *Kontaktsystem Inom Svenskt Navingsliv*, Gleerups, Lund (English summary: Contact systems in the Swedish Economy: a study of the external personal contacts of organizations).

HENDRICKSON, A. E. and WHITE, L. O. (1964) Promax: a quick method for rotation to oblique simple structure, *British Journal of Statistical Psychology* 17, 65-70.

HERMANSEN, T. (1968) Service trades and growth centres, in *Regional policy in EFTA*, European Free Trade Association, Geneva.

HERMANSEN, T. (1972) Development poles and development centres in national and regional development, in Kuklinski, A.R. (ed.), *Growth poles and growth centres in regional planning*, Mouton, The Hague.

HESSELING, P. (1970) Communication and organisational structure in a large multinational company, in Heald, G. (ed.), *Approaches to the study of organizational behaviour*, Tavistock, London.

HORST, P. (1965) *Factor analysis of data matrices*, Holt, Rinehart and Winston, New York.

ISARD, W. (1960) Industrial complex analysis, in *Methods of regional analysis*, MIT Press, Cambridge, Mass.

JANTSCH, E. (1967) *Technological forecasting in perspective*, O.E.C.D., Paris.

JOHNSTON, R. J. (1968) Choice in classification: the subjectivity of objective methods, *Annals of the Association of American Geographers* 58, 575-89.

JOHNSTON, R. J. (1970) Components analysis in geographical research, *Area* 4, 68-71.

LAZERFELD, P. F. and HENRY, N. W. (1968) The application of latent structure analysis to quantitative ecological data, in Massarik, F. and Ratoosh, P. (eds.), *Mathematical explorations in the behavioural sciencies*. Dorcey Press, Homewood, Illinois.

MACRAE, D. (1960) Direct factor analysis of sociometric data, *Sociometry* 23, 360-71.

MARDBERG, B. (1967) *Description of latent profile analysis program*, Swedish Council for Personnel Administration, Stockholm (mimeo).

MATTILLA, J. M. and THOMPSON, W. R. (1955) Measurement of the economic base of the metropolitan area, *Land Economics* 31, 160-68.

McCARTY, H. H., HOOK, J. C. and KNOS, D. S. (1956) *The measurement of association in industrial geography*, Department of Geography Report No. 1, State University of Iowa, Iowa.

McNAUGHTON-SMITH, T., *et al* (1964) Dissimilarity analysis: a new technique of hierarchical subdivision, *Nature* 202, 1034-5.

MORGAN, W. T. W. (1961) A functional approach to the study of office distributions, *Tijdschrift voor Economische en Sociale Geographie* 52, 207-10.

NEFT, D. (1966) *Statistical analysis for areal Distributions*, Monograph Series, No. 2, Regional Science Research Institute, Philadelphia.

PARKS, J. M. (1966) Cluster analysis applied to multivariate geological problems, *Journal of Geology.* 68, 703-15.

RAMSTROM, D. (1967) *The efficiency of control strategies*, Stockholm.

RANNELLS, J. (1956) *The core of the city*, University of Columbia Press, New York.

RHODES, J. and KAN, A. (1971) *Office dispersal and regional policy*, Occasional Paper No. 30, Department of Applied Economics, University of Cambridge.

RUSSETT, B. M. (1967) *International regions and the international system*, Rank McNally, New York.

SAHLBERG, B. (1969) *Inter Regionala Kontakt Monster*, Gleerup, Lund (English summary: Inter-regional contact flows).

SAVAGE, R. and DEUTSCH, K. W. (1960) A statistical model of the gross analysis of transaction flows, *Econometrica* 28, 551-72.

SHACHAR, A. (1967) Geostatistical techniques in urban research, *Regional Science Association Papers* 18, 197-206.

SIMON, H. A. (1960) *The shape of automation for men and management*, Harper Row, New York.

STEWART, R. (1967) *Managers and their jobs*, Macmillan, London.

THORNGREN, B. (1967) External economies and the urban core, in M. van Hulten, (ed.) *Urban core and inner city*, Brill, Leiden.

THORNGREN, B. (1970) How do contact systems affect regional development?, *Environment and Planning* 2, 409-27.

THORNGREN, B. (1972) KOMM-71: *Kommikationsunder-sokning vid statliga mydigheter*, Economics Research Institute, Stockholm School of Economics (mimeo). (English summary — communications between government agencies.)

THORNGREN, B. and GODDARD, J. B. (1973) *Groupings of government agencies through an analysis of contact flows*, Economics Research Institute, Stockholm School of Economics.

TRESS, R. C. (1938) Unemployment and diversification of industry, *The Manchester School* 9, 140-52.

TORNQVIST, G. (1970) *Contact systems and regional development*, Lund Studies in Geography, Series B, No. 35, Gleerup, Lund.

WEAVER, J. C. (1965) Crop combination regions in the Middlewest, *Geographical Review* 46, 536-65.

WEINSHALL, T. D. (1968) The communicogram, in J. R. Lawrence (ed.), *Operations research in the social sciences*, Tavistock, London.